HONEY

FROM HIVE TO HONEYPOT

A Celebration of Bees and Their Bounty

SUE STYLE

Illustrated by

GRAHAM EVERNDEN

CHRONICLE BOOKS

First published in the United States in 1993
by Chronicle Books.

Text copyright © 1992 by Sue Style
Illustrations copyright © 1992 by Graham Evernden

Designed by Janet James

ISBN: 0–8118–0286–8

Printed and bound in Italy by New Interlitho

Library of Congress Cataloging-in-Publication Data
available.

Distributed in Canada by Raincoast Books,
112 East Third Avenue, Vancouver, B.C. V5T 1C8.

10 9 8 7 6 5 4 3 2 1

Chronicle Books
275 Fifth Street
San Francisco, CA 94103

The author is grateful to the many people who helped her with this
book: Julian Johnston; Guy and Auguste Wittig; Romain Rey; Dr.
Elisha Burr Nyberg of Ciba Geigy SA; Erica Rokweiler; Colin Webb
and Helen Sudell of Pavilion Books; Caroline Herter and Carla
Charlton of Chronicle Books. The author and publisher are also grateful to the Estate of A. A. Milne and E. P. Dutton for permission to use
an extract from *Winnie-the-Pooh*.

CONTENTS

INTRODUCTION

Th'Industrious bee extracts from ev'ry flow'r
Its fragrant sweets, and mild balsamic pow'r.
Learn thence, with greatest care & nicest skill
To take the good, and to reject the ill:

By her example taught, enrich thy mind,
Improve kind nature's gifts, by sense refin'd;
Be thou the honey-comb – in whom may dwell
Each mental sweet, nor leave one vacant cell.

From a piece of embroidery by Sarah Ann Hitch, 1790,
quoted in Eva Crane's *The Archaeology of Beekeeping*.

Considering the fact that humans have been harvesting honey for at least the last 10,000 years, it would be understandable if by now we had become blasé about both the process and the product. Yet, the simple sense of wonder provoked by bees and their by-products is as great as it has ever been – perhaps even greater as people tire of urban life and hanker after the idea (if not the reality) of country living.

My own introduction to the industrious bee came when we fell in love with a small piece of the Sundgau countryside in southern Alsace. At the time the land housed a haphazard arrangement of hives, propped up against a bent old apple tree, their front doors gaily painted all colours of the rainbow. When we bought the land to build our own house, it was clear the bees were going to have to move theirs. In the autumn, when the honey season was over and the hives

quiet, they were discreetly removed to the old part of the village. The following spring the old apple tree fell down in a gale; it was as if the bees had never been. After we had moved in, I sat glorying in my new surroundings, feasting my eyes on meadows of wild flowers and enjoying distant, desk-bound views of some of the most beautiful forests in France. I began to wonder guiltily how our predecessors were faring.

Preliminary enquiries with my neighbour, Monsieur Auguste, were reassuring, as were the steady supplies of *miel toutes fleurs* (flower honey) and *miel de sapin* (pine honey) which found their sticky way into the letter-box or on to the doorstep. It seemed the bees were none the worse for their ordeal, and were continuing to go about their business in their characteristically efficient and untroubled way. Once I had expressed an interest, regular invitations to witness important events in their life began to punctuate my calm summer days. When a May swarm loomed over the horizon and installed itself in Monsieur Auguste's tree, we assembled at a respectful distance and watched admiringly as this sprightly septuagenarian donned his veil, shinned up his fruit-picking ladder, swiftly swept the whole heaving, humming mass into his swarming box and snapped the top shut.

A few weeks later, shaking a sorrowing head, he voiced the alarming suspicion that a queen bee had gone AWOL from one of his hives; the situation must immediately be remedied by introducing a new queen, otherwise the whole colony might self-destruct. Periodically there would be signs of great activity down in the *cave*: out popped a head and I was bidden to watch the battered extractor at work. One by one, the frames were scraped of wax, inserted into vertical holders, the handle cranked, the whole thing whizzed around like a salad spinner and the honey thrown against the sides of the drum. Out the bottom it came, then into drums where it was left to mature. Later Madame Auguste would pot it up in jars ready for sale. Odd scrapings of wax and well-used comb were carefully melted down and sent over to Dannemarie for re-cycling into foundation. There was never a dull moment.

Little by little, honey insinuated itself into our lives. From simply piling it onto *baguettes* bought still warm from the baker's daily delivery van, or onto yogurt home-made from the creamy milk fetched fresh from the farm, we progressed to warm salads enlivened with a splash of honey vinegar, chicken pieces sweetly marinated for the barbecue with a honey and spice paste, and lamb with dried fruits and a honeyed finish. Even puddings – rare in our household – began to make an appearance. Honey is so much more interesting than sugar, and anyway (we reasoned), as everyone knows, Honey Is Good For You.

One thing seemed to lead to another. I began to be curious about the history of bee-keeping and of the domestication of the honey bee; what the bees get up to in the hive, and what keeps the bee-keeper busy. Then came the burning question: is honey *actually* good for you? Or, is it simply good to eat? And finally, what does it taste of, or is it simply sweet? By now we were happily installed in our new house. It was time to enrich my mind and get busy on a book about honey

Sue Style · Bettlach, Alsace · March 1992

Of
HONEY AND BEES

What is sweeter than honey?
What is more pure or more nourishing?
It is the milk of the aged, it prolongs their existence, and when
they descend into the tomb, it still serves to embalm them.

Alexis Soyer *The Pantropheon* 1853

In a painting in the Spider Cave at La Arana, eastern Spain, which dates back about 8,000 years, a lithe figure is depicted clinging precariously to a branch. She holds a basket in one hand, while the other is plunged deeply into what looks like a sixties beehive hair-do. All around there are unmistakeable signs of intense insect activity. From such graphic evidence it is clear that man was busy tracking down bees' nests and cutting out the honeycombs many thousands of years ago. And though honey harvesting is no longer quite so hazardous, man's predilection for pinching honey from the bees is as pronounced as ever.

The love poetry of the Sumerians shows that honey was no stranger to this earliest of civilizations: "more fragrant than honey" are the caresses of the bride, while the King's bedchamber is "filled with honey". The Babylonians appear to have been fond of a delicious-sounding sort of breakfast spread: rich cream or sour milk mixed with flour, sesame seeds, dates and honey. Doubtless the Hanging Gardens were filled with the buzz of Babylonian bees, though they

would certainly have been wild ones for it was to be a
another few thousand years before it occurred to man to
house his bees in some sort of hive. It would be difficult to
overestimate the significance of honey to the ancient Egyptians: the fullest and most graphic accounts of bee-keeping
in ancient times come from Egyptian tombs, where the first
recorded hives can be seen. In many hieroglyphs the bee
represents royalty, while honey was considered a food first
for gods and then for humans. It was extensively used in
cosmetics but above all for medical purposes. And when the
Pharaohs descended finally into the tomb, it served to
embalm them.

In India, where sugar was certainly known from a very
early date, honey nevertheless managed to more than hold
its own and was vested with reli-
gious as well as royal significance.
Honey was the first food of the
Hindu god Indra, and bees formed
the string of the bow belonging to
Kama, the god of love; and kings
were anointed with honey before
coronation.

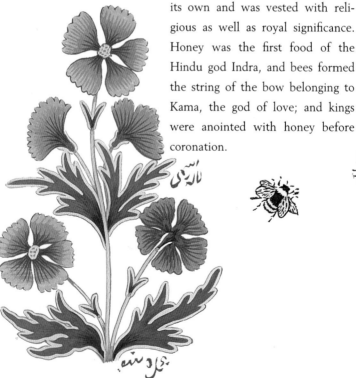

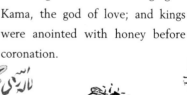

Honey accompanied Indian people from the cradle to the grave. It was included in the first food of a newborn infant; it figured in marriage ceremonies (some claim our word "honeymoon" is linked to this practice) and an offering of honey and ghee (clarified butter) was reserved for the dead. It seems that the strict Hindu dietary laws which limit the free exchange of foods between castes make an exception for honey, which may be accepted by anyone. Their *madhu* (honey wine) has given us the word "mead".

Old Testament references to honey are legion, from the oft-quoted "land flowing with milk and honey" to the exhortation in Proverbs to "eat honey, my son, for it is good; honey from the comb is sweet to your taste." Wild bees made their nest in the rib-cage of the lion killed by Samson so that "out of the strong came forth sweetness", and the manna which sustained the Israelites in the wilderness is thought to have been a type of honeydew.

The ancient Greeks made extensive use of honey in salves and potions, in prepared dishes, to make perfume, as libations for the dead, and to appease the gods. Bee-keepers numbered among their ranks the philosopher Aristotle; for Hippocrates, the father of medicine, honey was a favourite remedy. The followers of Pythagoras lived on a diet of bread and honey – and seemed to far outlive any of their contemporaries. Such was the position of bees (and their keepers) in Greek society that they had their own special patron-god, Aristaeus. According to legend, he was the son of Apollo and the nymph Cyrene, and came from Malta (formerly known as Melita – "honey island"), where he was brought up by nymphs who taught him a number of useful skills: how to curdle milk (to make cheese), how to cultivate olives (to make oil) and how to keep bees (to make honey).

The Romans, too, were enthusiastic and efficient apiarists. Pliny and Virgil all wrote extensively about bees and honey, the latter devoting his entire fourth book of *The Georgics* to the subject. Interestingly, in spite of its wide use, people were still unclear about how honey (or indeed bees) actually happened. Virgil talks of "the heavenly gift of honey from the air", while Pliny refers to "the perspiration of the sky or a sort of saliva of the stars."

There was considerable confusion also about sex and gender. Virgil was under the impression bees "forbear to indulge in copulation or to enervate their bodies in Venus' ways, nor do they bear their young in travail, but themselves, unmated, gather their children in their mouths from leaves and fragrant herbs, themselves supply their king and infant citizens and recreate their halls and waxen kingdoms." Though there seemed to be a vague understanding that the quality of honey was related to the quality of the flowers in which it was stored, it was to be at least 1,000 years before the crucial relationship between flowers and bees became clear. Even in the seventeenth century, Charles II's court bee-keeper, Moses Rusden, was under the illusion that queen bees were kings and that workers were sexless (though this may simply have been prudent politics on his part, given a male monarch recently restored). Over drones he drew a veil. And it was not until the nineteenth century that the puzzle of how bees reproduce themselves was properly understood.

The Romans would certainly have considered *mulsum* a fermented drink consisting of grape juice or young wine mixed with honey to be among heaven's gifts. Pliny recounts that when one of his friends was asked how he had achieved the ripe old age of 100 years, he answered: "*Mulsum* within and oil without!" Apicius, in his famous cook book, manages to include honey in almost half of the 468-odd recipes. Even truffles get the honey treatment. Should the Roman conscience start to prick a little at all this self-indulgence, honey could always be used in sacrifices to placate the deities.

The early Christians inherited much of the Greek and Roman reverence for honey, and added their own wisdom to it. According to one legend, the worker bee was blessed on leaving the Garden of Eden with the title of "handmaid of the Lord", like Mary, with whom she seemed to share the distinction of a virgin birth. (Since bees did not appear to have sexual intercourse, the analogy was frequently drawn in the early days between the bee family and the Holy Family.)

Byzantine civilization also accorded a place of honour to the bee, likening it to the soul because of its purity and its

habit of always coming home to rest. The souls of the dead were thought to come back from the moon to the earth where they were reincarnated in the form of bees. Muhammad, who forbade his followers wine, urged them to consume honey instead: "Eat honey my son, for it is good, not only to eat but against all kind of illness." The Koran contains many references to the importance of bees and the soothing powers of honey, for "there cometh forth from their bellies a drink diverse of hues, wherein is healing for mankind."

Bees were sacred to the Mayas of the Yucatan peninsula of Mexico, and bee-keeping activity, rather as in ancient Greece, came under the aegis of its own special god. A dead bee found in the path of a wandering Maya would be accorded a simple burial service and carefully covered with leaves. Some centuries later, Quetzalcoatl, the Aztec god of fertility, was pictured on his travels accompanied by bees.

For the early Teutonic peoples, the Celts and the Slavs, honey was once again food for the gods, while mead was a drink much indulged in by mere mortals. The Icelandic god Odin was said to owe his strength and wisdom to the mystical powers of honey. The purity of bees was revered and respected, to the extent that a woman was not permitted to keep bees because of her monthly "uncleanness". Also forbidden was any sort of argument in the presence of bees; modern bee-keepers still believe firmly that these sensitive insects will not thrive in the company of a quarrelsome family. "Telling the bees" is another interesting old custom common to most of northern Europe and which persists to this day (in Yorkshire, at least). When the bee-keeper died, the bees had to be told of his death otherwise they too would die. Less commonly other family events of note were also told to the bees, indicating the special place of honour they held in the family:

Marriage, birth or burying,
News across the seas,
All your sad or merrying
You must tell the bees.

In Frankish times, the bee as royal motif crops up again: in the tomb of King Childerich (excavated in Tournai cathedral in 1653) 300 solid gold bees mounted on rings, which had once embellished the royal cape, were found. (They were later used by Napoleon to embellish his.)

Monasteries throughout Europe in the Middle Ages (then as now) were actively engaged in the fabrication and use of honey for the kitchen and the medicine chest, and beeswax for the chapel. In the tenth century, we find Brother Ekkehard at the Abbey of St. Gallen, in eastern Switzerland, carefully chronicling the monks' menus, while from the Leech Book of Glastonbury Abbey, in England, we learn that the good brothers counselled on the use of honey not only as medicine for the body but also for a broken heart. Judging by the wild fluctuations in honey harvests recorded year by year, bee-keeping was no more predictable then than it is now. Doubtless the old monks shook their sorry heads in the Abbey bee garden, bemoaning the fact that things were not what they used to be and mourning the good old days when the weather was kind and the nectar flowed. (Talk to a bee-keeper today and you will get the same message.)

Throughout the Middle Ages, beeswax continued to be an important item of church and household supplies. Some of

the world's finest statues (including Cellini's Perseus with the head of Medusa) were cast using the so-called lost wax technique: the figure was made first of beeswax, then coated with a fireproof material, heated until the wax melted and the resulting cavity filled with molten metal. Honey continued to be an essential component of any self-respecting housewife's pharmacopoeia. Above all it was still the only available sweetening agent and played a vital part in all the old-established medieval specialities like gingerbread, *Lebkuchen* (spice cake), *Leckerli* (spiced Swiss pastry), *Hypokras* (spiced red wine) and *pain d'épices* (spiced bread).

From the sixteenth century onwards, sugar, extracted first from cane and later from beet, became the universal, cheap sweetener. Honey began to seem an expensive luxury. Its star began to fade.

Now, as people once again realize there is a great deal more to honey than simple sweetness, this ancient product of nature looks set to regain its rightful, natural place in the scheme of things.

From the HIVE TO THE HONEYPOT

*The hives themselves, whether you like them stitched of hollow
cork or woven of pliant osiers, must have their entrance narrow:
winter's grip solidifies the honey; summer's heat dissolves it into
liquid. For the bees either extreme is harmful . . . But you your-
self should plaster with smooth clay to keep them snug those
chunky dormitories, and apply a coat of leaves to finish. Let no
yew be found too near the hive. Let no red crab be roasted on
your hearth. Avoid a bog or place of stinking slime, or where the
voice rebounds in the hollow echo from the rocks.*

Virgil (70–19 BC)
The Georgics, Book Four, translated by L. P. Wilkinson.

oney is as old as the hills, while hives developed
only gradually as the honey hunter turned bee-
keeper and started looking around for ways of making his life
easier. In the centuries preceding Virgil's pertinent advice on
the construction and siting of hives, honey gathering had
been a rather hit-and-miss affair. Wild nests were sited
somewhat inconveniently – as witnessed in the cave paintings in eastern Spain and in Africa – wherever the bees
wished to alight, rather than where the apiarist chose to put
them. Besides the inaccessibility of the hives, another problem was that often the only way for the honey hunter to get
at his spoils was to tear apart the whole edifice, thereby

destroying the colony – and getting severely stung in the process. Little by little, *Homo sapiens* tumbled to the idea of housing bees in a place of their own choosing.

The earliest recorded hives specifically built to house the honey bee are found in ancient Egyptian paintings dating from 2,500 BC. From the evidence on the walls of the tomb of Rekhmire ("Tomb 100") at Thebes about a century later, it is clear the Egyptians had progressed from simple raids on wild nests to the systematic removal of honey from man-made hives, albeit fairly primitive ones. Hollow tubes made from a mixture of mud and wattle were baked in the hot sun of the Nile basin, then superimposed, lined up like a log pile and the interstices filled with clay. Inside, the bees made their own careful – but still rather inaccessible – arrangement of wax combs variously filled with developing bees, pollen and honey.

The cylindrical idea was adopted by both the Greeks and the Romans. Over the centuries horizontal hives continued to have their supporters, particularly in southern areas, while their more northerly bee-keeping brothers preferred to stand their hives upright. Materials were local: mud or baked clay in the southern Mediterranean, cane in China and Ethiopia, wicker or straw in northern Europe, cork from the Iberian peninsula. Hollow tree trunks were widely used in the forested areas of northern and eastern Europe.

What with the problems of wild bees and wild bears, the man-made hive – however primitive – certainly had some advantages. The main snag was that having persuaded the bees to go into the hive, how could the bee-keeper get the bee-built honeycombs out, which the bees by then had firmly welded to the walls and often to the ceiling? Horizontal hives were the easiest: for these, bee-keepers developed a system of smoking the bees into the front end and retrieving some honeycombs from the back without the need to destroy the colony. Getting honey from an upright hive was a less simple matter. It was distressingly common practice to break it open or tip it over at the end of the season and to sulphur (or drown) the bees to get at the spoils. A few colonies would be left to over-winter, thereby at least ensuring something to start with the following year. But basically it was the old story of killing the goose that laid the golden egg. The time was ripe for something more flexible — and more humane.

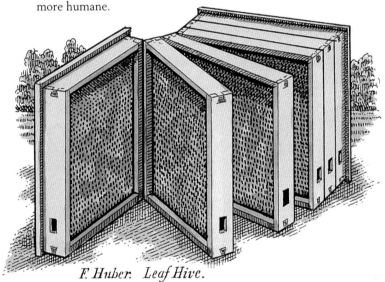

F. Huber. Leaf Hive.

In 1792, François Huber, a Swiss naturalist and bee-keeper, invented the so-called leaf hive. He provided wooden frames hinged together like the leaves of a book in which the bees built their combs. The end leaves were of glass, enabling others (though not Huber himself, for he was blind) to observe the process of comb-building and general bee busy-ness in the hive. For a number of years Huber's hive, though suffering from some quite serious drawbacks, was greatly valued for the lessons it offered in watching bees at work. As the nineteenth century dawned, bee people all over Europe with designs on hives, from the Silesian-born Dr. Dzierzon to the French Monsieur Debeauvoys, from the German Baron von Berlepsch to the British Mr. Munn, went to work to produce improvements and refinements.

The various frame hives they invented, though an advance on what had gone before, still shared one fundamental flaw. The problem was that sooner or later the bees thoughtlessly immobilized the frames by gumming up the spaces between them with propolis or wax. It took a Pennsylvania pastor rejoicing in the name of Lorenzo Lorraine Langstroth to come up with a solution which changed the face of modern bee-keeping. He is generally credited with the important discovery in 1851 of "bee space", though others (including Huber) certainly knew of it. This magic dimension – one quarter to three-eighths of an inch (six to ten millimetres) – corresponds approximately to the vital statistics of the average bee. Such a space left around all the movable parts in the hive gave the bee enough room to move about freely between frames, but not enough to fill the space with propolis or to build comb in it and thus render the frame immobile.

So excited was Langstroth by the implications of his discovery that he could apparently scarcely restrain himself from dashing out into the street shouting "Eureka!" He went on to design a hive in which all the frames were (and remained) completely movable because the concept of bee

*Langstroth's
Movable-frame.*

space had been recognized and respected. "The use of these frames will, I am persuaded" he wrote modestly in his diary in 1851, "give a new impetus to the easy and profitable management of bees". The implications for modern bee-keeping were, in fact, immense.

Langstroth's breakthrough stimulated a whole generation of yet more fanciful blueprints, and hive design reached something of a crescendo in the second half of the nineteenth century. Some, like Dadant's (a Frenchman who later emigrated to the U.S.), which followed closely on Langstroth's have stood the test of time. Others enjoyed a brief burst of fame, but their usefulness proved to be limited. A glorious example was Monsieur Eldy-Gorlier's beautiful twenty-four compartment glass-fronted observa-

tion hive which doubtless elicited gasps of admiration at the Paris Exhibition of 1878. Another was the British Mr. Nutt's collateral hive. They were works of art, probably of limited use to the apiarist, but much recommended as garden ornaments or as conversation pieces. Some were even kept indoors.

Eldy~Gorlier   Observation Hive.

Nowadays, hives remain delightfully diverse, though those with a mind for standardization might wish it otherwise. Each new hive always claims to be the answer to every bee-keeper's prayer and to offer untold advantages over all of its predecessors. Bees, meanwhile, clearly don't mind too much since they will nest happily in a hollow tree trunk given half a chance.

The logical sequel to the fully movable frame hive was the invention of pre-formed wax comb foundation to be fitted into the movable wooden frame. It effectively permitted far higher yields of honey than had previously been possible, for without it bees waste precious time in the short honey season building their own honeycomb from scratch. In 1857, a German gentleman named Mehring had the clever idea of fabricating wax sheets which bore the hexagonal imprint of a natural bee cell. Others, both in the United States and in

Britain, did a bit of fine tuning on Mehring's original design, and soon wax sheets were being turned out mechanically by the thousands. All that remained for the bees to do was to knead and soften the comb, and to draw it out to a sufficient depth to receive eggs or pollen. At around the same time, Abbé Collin in France invented the queen excluder, a sort of grille placed above the hive's nursery quarters where the brood nest was situated. It prevented the queen from laying eggs in the upper storeys or supers. Surplus honey could thus be kept in a separate compartment from developing bees with their own stocks of food; it was easier to extract and the bees were left undisturbed.

Hand in hand with the arrival of the movable frame hive filled with wax comb foundation came the invention of the honey extractor. The inspiration for the idea is said to have come to its inventor Francesco de Hruschka, a major in the Imperial Austrian army, after he had idly observed his son

swinging some honeycomb around his head in a basket. (Presumably the honey shot out of the sides.) The basic principle which he developed involved hanging the frames vertically inside a drum and spinning them round so that the centrifugal force threw the honey out to sides of the drum, and it then trickled down and was recuperated at the bottom. It was the final piece in the puzzle of how best to get the honey from the hive to the honey-pot.

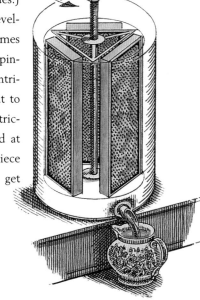

The BUSY BEE

How doth the little busy bee
Improve each shining hour
And gather honey all the day
From every opening flower.
How skilfully she builds her cell,
How neat she spreads the wax,
And labours hard to store it well
With the sweet food she makes.

Against Idleness and Mischief Isaac Watts

As you recline idly on your picnic rug in the middle of a meadow full of wild flowers alive with bees, or watch one of them burying itself in the deepest recesses of a rose in your front garden, it is impossible not to wonder at the purposeful busyness of this little insect. Where did she come from? What is she after? Where is she going next? How will she find her way home? And anyway, how do we know she's a "she"?

If you were to follow her home and into her hive, in the darkness you would dimly distinguish row upon row of wooden frames arranged vertically in a box, like files hanging in a cabinet. Enclosed by each frame you would find a miraculous wax construction, upon both sides of which your bee friend and her comrades would have tirelessly worked to

form cells – a sort of back-to-back hexagonal housing unit for honey, pollen and bees in various stages of their development. In the lower part of the honeycomb you would see cells inhabited apparently by a small dot, or a tiny worm.

Roof

Glass quilt

Super with frames

Queen excluder

Brood box with frames

Floor with entrance block

Some of the cells would be sealed over with wax. In a swathe above them, there would be some cells filled with brightly coloured specks of pollen. Still higher up, the cells would be full of glistening honey, some of them capped with wax. Over the surface of each of the frames, on both sides, bees would be moving in an incessant rhythmical pattern. On closer inspection, you might distinguish three different types of bee: small, neat, agile little bodies like the one you followed home from the fields (workers); big, hairy, heavily built insects seemingly without gainful employ (drones); you might even spot a single, smooth, elongated silhouette purposefully bobbing her elegant body by turns into each of the cells (the queen bee).

Queen.

Worker.

Whether worker, drone or queen, the bee in question belongs to the race *Apis mellifera* or *mellifica*. (Linnaeus first qualified it as *mellifera*, honey-bearing. Later, when he realized that the bee actually made the honey in the hive, he changed the qualification to *mellifica* – honey-making. English- and French-speakers tend to stick to *mellifera*; in German and other languages, *mellifica* is preferred.) Otherwise known as the domestic honey bee, it occurs naturally throughout Africa, Europe and the Middle East, and has been exported by man

Drone.

with varying degrees of success to other parts of the globe. The encyclopaedia describes it rather endearingly as a social bee. This does not imply that it is a great party-goer (though admittedly it goes in for some pretty impressive dance routines inside the hive), but rather that it conforms to an astonishingly well-organized system of government. There is talk of a clearly defined caste system;

certainly every bee seems to know its place and is in it when necessary. When no longer required, it either retires gracefully or is thrown out. An admirable – if ruthless – way of managing society which, in the case of bees, works to perfection.

At the hub of the hive's activity is the queen, also known as the mother bee, even on occasions as the king bee. Bee people consider that the term "mother bee" is more accurate – if less glamorous – than "queen bee". They point out that she does nothing to actually direct the operations of the hive, she simply fulfils the task prescribed for her by her workers: that of laying eggs and making babies at the right time and in the right place.

Queen or simple matriarch, she is certainly born to the role, brought up in a special cell in the back-to-back housing unit, hatched out, permanently guarded by a dozen or so ladies-in-waiting who stroke, lick, touch and feed her with special food – royal jelly. Generally speaking, there will be only one queen bee in a hive. In the whole of her three- to four-year life span, she has but one brief moment of glory when the time for her nuptial flight arrives – unless rain stops play, in which case even this small but significant sortie is denied her. If all goes according to plan, in the warmth of a summer afternoon she soars high above the hive, hotly pursued by a handful of hopeful drones whose job is to mate with her for once and for all. In her small but specially elongated body will be stored, as a result of the mating, a cool four to five million sperm cells – the potential for enough bee babies to last her whole life through and to see the hive through several seasons. The drones' task completed (and significant parts of their anatomy irrevocably damaged), they die from their exertions.

The queen retreats to her hive for a lifetime of laying. Over the years, guided by her court, she works her way steadily over as many combs as are put before her. In some cells she deposits fertilized eggs which will become workers or possibly queens (females); in other, larger cells, unfertilized eggs which will develop into drones (males). You can hardly blame her – though bee-keepers tend to – for wanting to swarm once in a while, the only other opportunity she has to get out and have a bit of fun. Otherwise she will be there until she dies on the job, or is early retired by her peers or by the bee-keeper, or killed by the cruel dart of a challenging new queen who thinks she can do better.

Surrounding the queen in huge numbers are the worker bees, who typically make up about ninety-five per cent of the hive's population. They are the ones you most often see out and about – and incidentally, the ones most likely to sting you. (The queen bee has a sting but rarely uses it, and then only on other hapless insects; drones have no sting.)

Once hatched out, they proceed to clean themselves and the cell from which they have emerged. They then go straight to work as nurse bees, keeping the nursery quarters warm, feeding the developing bee babies and receiving nectar from incoming workers. Their next job is to pack pollen into the cells and keep things spick and span. At around ten days old they start to secrete wax, soften it with their jaws and use it to build wax cells. Some of them are detailed to surround the queen like courtiers, as she makes her royal progress over the face of the comb. They feed her special food and take from her a hormonal substance which they distribute throughout the hive. The drones also need to be fed, since they cannot go out to forage for themselves.

Finally the workers' duties take them outside where they act as guard bees by the hive entrance, and air conditioners, fanning their wings to keep things cool. Still only halfway through their short life, they set off to scout for and collect pollen and nectar. With such a programme of feeding and foraging, it is little wonder that at the height of summer the worker bee's life span is so short. Only those born towards the end of the season have a longer life cycle. They will survive the winter, ready to get briefly busy the following spring on the all-important task of grooming their successor bees, then die out, too, in their turn.

Lolling about on the sidelines during the summer months are the somewhat underemployed, overfed males, the drones ("that pack of shirkers", Virgil called them). They cannot go out to forage for nectar, but instead take their rations from the home-coming workers, or directly from the cells. If the afternoon is particularly warm and inviting, they might hover about above the hive hoping for a passing queen to dash out on her nuptial flight: their main role in life is to mate with the queen, though they do also keep the home fires (figuratively) burning in the hive when all the workers are out looking for food. Since but a handful of the couple of hundred drones which inhabit the hive will end up being lucky suitors, they have a hard time justifying their existence. As if to compound their image problem, they have no father, only a poor overworked mother. At the end of the summer, their fellow workers count up the winter stocks and enumerate the hungry mouths to be fed through the months to come. The drones' number is up; they are either summarily stung to death or chased out of the hive to die of starvation.

The real business of the hive appears to the unitiated to begin in the spring. As soon as the temperature outside reaches a certain level, some worker bees will venture out in search of stocks of pollen and nectar to boost the hive's fast-dwindling winter stores.

The foraging bee which has been out scouting for nectar stocks returns to the hive to pass on the good news to her fellow workers. This information will be given in the form of a dance, observed over the years by many people but only properly understood and interpreted in the 'twenties by Prof. Karl Ritter von Frisch in Bavaria. First there is the Round Dance, and then there is the Waggle (or Wagtail) Dance. In the former, which is used when the food source is fairly close to the hive, the bee dashes round in a circle on the face of the honeycomb, then turns round and repeats the performance in the opposite direction. Soon she is joined on the dance floor by other bees who follow her movements to get the gist of her message, as well as picking up the scent of the nectar source.

The Waggle Dance is used to indicate that the nectar supplies are more than 100 yards (100 metres) from the hive. Here the bee does a more intricate set of steps, waggling her body; the more sustained the performance, the more significant the nectar source. She can even tell her fellow workers which angle to fly from the direction of the sun. Though Prof. von Frisch was awarded the Nobel Prize for interpreting the intricacies of the dances, the bees surely deserve some credit for having devised such a brilliant routine in the first place.

Thus, fired with enthusiasm, a worker sets out from the hive on a mission which may take her anywhere within about a 3 mile (5 kilometre) radius of the hive. On each flight (of which in the height of summer she may make up to twenty five a day) she will visit only one sort of flower. This phenomenon, known as "flower fidelity", is nature's neat way of not confusing the pollination issue. She plunges her

head deep into the centre of the chosen bloom, picking up in the process quite a lot of pollen on her hairy little body and transferring it to the stigma of the flower. She also keeps a little for herself. (Bees have six legs, and store pollen in the back pair.) With her proboscis, she sucks up the nectar (or honeydew) and stores it in her honey sac, ready to take it home to the hive. And so she continues from flower to flower and tree to tree, giving and receiving, ensuring fruit for the farmer, food for her family and honey for us.

Once fully laden, she scurries back to the hive via the shortest route – hence the expression "making a bee-line" for somewhere. In her honey sac is semi-digested nectar, and pollen is stored down her little legs. At the entrance to the hive, she will be met by guard bees, standing watch to fight off marauding wasps or hornets, or empty-handed bees from another hive which could be construed as potential robbers. Generally speaking, only the bees which belong to that colony will be allowed in, anything else may be savagely set upon and stung to death. She passes on her load of nectar to another worker bee who will further work on it to gradually reduce its water content from around three-quarters of its weight to less than a quarter. Its complex sugar (sucrose) is also converted into simpler ones (glucose and fructose). Alternatively, the foraging worker may deposit the nectar herself in an empty cell. Pollen, the bees' protein which is essential for the rearing of the brood, is also packed into cells, moistened to a paste with water.

At certain times of the year she may carry home propolis, also known as "bee glue", gleaned from sticky buds and leaves. This unique substance is used to shore up any cracks or holes, for bees are firm about requiring only one entrance to their hive. To create any additional air inlet would be like opening a window in an air-conditioned house in Miami in mid-summer. Any cracks or holes which appear to threaten this carefully balanced ventilation system are therefore promptly sealed up with propolis by the bees. At the entrance to the hive are rows of bees, stationed in strict formation, whose sole job is to create a draught system by fanning their wings vigorously and tirelessly. The warm, moist air of the hive is sucked out one side of the hole, the fresh cool air is pumped in the other and the temperature is kept stable. Propolis is also used to embalm foreign bodies. In winter, for example, mice have been known to find their way into hives and sometimes die on the premises. The body is too big for the bees to drag out, so it is immediately embalmed in bee glue to prevent putrefaction.

At the height of summer when the nectar is in full flow, the queen should by rights be in residence and busily fulfilling her motherhood duties. If she is in her second or third summer, her laying capacity may become a little erratic and eggs will be deposited all over the place, rather than concentrated in one area. Her workers will discreetly make arrangements to replace her by building some specially designed queen cells, little wombs for future queens, considerably larger than normal cells and often hanging from the lower edge of the comb. Once a new queen is born, the dowager will be quietly despatched and the business of the hive will go on undisturbed. This process is called supersedure.

Much more disruptive to hive life (and thus to honey production) is the unexpected death of a queen – squashed on removal of a frame, perhaps. Then the alarm signal goes up and a well-rehearsed emergency plan swings into action. Soon three or four normal hexagonal cells on the face of the comb will be specially enlarged and rounded out by the worker bees. The resident larvae, which would ordinarily develop into plain workers, will – by dint of special rations of royal jelly – develop the characteristics of the queen bee. Once hatched out, one of them will take precedence over all the others, whom she will proceed to kill with well-armed stings. True to her instincts, the virgin queen will set off on her nuptial flight, then settle down to the interrupted task of populating the hive.

An alternative scenario to that of supercedure or accidental death of a queen is that of swarming. In the early summer when the nectar begins to flow in earnest, there is something of a population explosion in the hive. In a matter of weeks, the numbers can increase from 10,000 to 40,000. Scouts are then sent off in search of a new home; a high-pitched piping sound can be heard in the hive; much agitated activity is observed outside. One day, as if at a given signal, out of the front entrance streams a seething mass of bee life which

soars up into the sky followed by a scrambling, frantic crowd of hangers-on. The swarm, by now a ballooning, swaying mass of workers clustered around its queen, comes first to rest fairly near the hive – which gives the vigilant bee-keeper the chance to run for his swarming box and sweep the bees inside, later to re-house them in an empty hive where there is plenty of room for them to breed and store nectar and pollen. Otherwise, they take wing again and set off for their permanent (previously reconnoitred) home – a hollow tree trunk, perhaps, or some sort of crevice or cave.

As summer draws to a close, the feverish activity of the hive begins to calm down. Any workers born now should survive the winter – a strong hive full of healthy bees with late summer birthdays is important to the survival of the colony for next spring. The last harvest of honey is removed, and the bees receive a feed of sugar syrup in return, to nourish them through the months to come. The drones have long since departed and as winter draws on, the workers wisely retreat to the middle of the comb and snuggle up around the queen. Bees, contrary to popular opinion, do not hibernate, they simply lie low and cuddle up close to conserve warmth and energy.

Once or twice in the depths of winter, when the temperature goes above 46°–50°F (10°–12°C) and the watery rays of sunlight delude them into thinking spring is just around the corner, the bees come out to do their business. Soon the queen resumes her laying programme in readiness for the busy days of early spring when the nectar begins to flow. The bee-keeper's year starts in earnest.

The BEE KEEPER'S YEAR

The bees have their definite plan for life, perfected through countless ages, and nothing you can do will ever turn them from it. You can delay their work, or you can even thwart it altogether, but no one has ever succeeded in changing a single principle in bee-life. And so the best bee-master is always the one who most exactly obeys the orders from the hive.

The Bee-master of Warrilow, Tickner Edwards 1920

The bee-keeper starts to take his orders from the hive in the spring. According to an old English tradition, it falls to St. Gregory to open up the flowers on March 12, while on March 21, St. Benedict summons the bees from their hives to search for nectar. The apiarist reaches down his hat and veil from the shelf, fetches his smoker, his goose feather quill and his hive tools and sets off to see how his bees have fared during the winter. What does he hope to

find? The first reassuring sign is plenty of bee activity at the hive entrance. A large number of disembodied heads and wings outside the hive spells trouble: perhaps there has been a winter visit from a shrew-mouse whose little corpse may be inside, mummified by the meticulous bees. Carefully he

Net Veil

Bent Nose Smoker

removes the roof of the hive and peels away the sacking. Slight stirrings are heard. He lifts out one of the frames with a pincer-like instrument and gives a few gentle puffs on a smoker, causing the bees to take in stocks of food so they become less aggressive. Using the goose feather, he gently brushes away any bees still clinging to the frame. With a grunt of satisfaction he notes that the queen has been busy for at least a month: some cells are already filled with developing bees, others with recently laid eggs. Stocks of food are still good. Quickly and quietly he returns everything to its proper place and closes the hive.

About a month later on a warm spring day, the bee-keeper can permit himself a more thorough inspection. A well-centred area of cells nicely stocked with eggs and larvae glistening like mother-of-pearl ("the brood nest") and extending over several central frames tells him the hive is humming and the queen is in full spate. Surrounding them in a sort of halo there should also be some cells filled with honey and pollen ("bee bread"), for there will be a run on these vital foodstuffs during the next few weeks when the nectar begins to flow. And the hive should be well-populated with healthy, busy workers. From the floor of the hive the bee-keeper removes any accumulated wax or propolis, dead bees and other debris.

It would be too much for the bee-keeper to hope that all his colonies had survived the rigours of winter without mishap. Some hives may be short of food, others short of inhabitants, still others will have lost their queen. For those which seem to be going hungry, a feed may be provided in the form of honey or sugar syrup. Weak hives will later be united with stronger ones, queenless ones re-queened. The bee-keeper must not forget that his bees also need water: an old window-box filled with damp moss or a seeping hosepipe peppered with holes placed close to the hive does the trick nicely.

Completing his inspection (the results of which he will probably record in a battered old notebook), the bee-keeper re-inserts any frames removed at the end of the summer. Old, blackened comb is replaced with pristine new wax sheets, which are put in next to the brood nest to give the bees nice clean nursery quarters. In due course, upper storeys ("supers") and/or extra frames may be added so the bees can continue to extend themselves outwards and upwards from their tight winter cluster. In these early days, the bee-master keeps a weather eye on the spring skies – these can be hazardous times for a newly overwintered colony if its food stocks are already dwindling. Prematurely warm spring weather can provoke the hive to go all out with its breeding programme, but a sudden subsequent spell of cold or rain will keep the bees inside, unable to go out and fetch food for all those newborn bee babies. Then, says my neighbour Monsieur Auguste, *le murmure de la grande récolte* (the murmur of the great harvest) goes up – a great mournful buzzing of hungry bees – and the only answer may be to feed them a little syrup to stave off starvation.

Late spring is the time when a bee's fancy tends to turn inconveniently to thoughts of swarming – an instinct which, for all man's claims to have domesticated the honey bee, he has by no means suppressed. Why do bees swarm? There may be too little room in the hive, or there may be insufficient space left to store honey; it may simply be too hot in there, or perhaps there is an old queen whose time has come. The fact is, however, that since no-one really knows what actually triggers the swarming instinct, all the bee-keeper can do is to take preventive measures. He can provide more room by adding extra frames or more supers; over the years he can keep track of his queens, marking them with coloured markers and replacing them

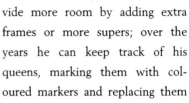

Supers

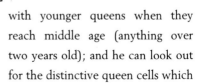

with younger queens when they reach middle age (anything over two years old); and he can look out for the distinctive queen cells which show that a hive is getting ready to swarm, and nip them in the bud.

But if all these precautions fail, *le chant de la reine* ("the queen's song", a curious piping sound emitted by the queen before swarming) goes up and the bees take flight. Then the bee-keeper should be on hand to follow them and fetch them home, for their first resting place will be quite near the hive before they proceed to their final, previously reconnoitred site.

Swarming has given rise to many an old dictum: *un essaim du mois de mai vaut une vache à lait* say the French ("a swarm of bees in May is worth a dairy cow"), while in Germany *ein Schwarm in Mai* brings *ein Fuder Heu*. For British bee-keepers as well as for German ones, a swarm in May is worth a load of hay. All of which presuppose that you are the lucky one to find and claim the swarm, rather than the one from whose hives they have flown. It is a bitter thing for a bee-keeper to bear when he has lovingly tended his hives and built up the colony during the year, only to have them all buzz off.

Wherever and whenever it happens, swarming can be a bit of a bind for bee-keepers, bringing headaches and hazards. The greatest of these is not, as you might suppose, bee stings – bees seldom sting when swarming because they have filled themselves with food before setting off on their journey – but broken limbs. Once the swarm is safely boxed, the bee-keeper leaves it in a cool place until the evening. Then he must decide what to do with it. If the bees have left behind them a seriously depleted hive, he may want to send them back again whence they came. He lays an old rug on the ground and shakes them out on to it. On hands and knees he searches carefully for the queen and removes her. The homeless bees, sensing that they have lost their mother, troop back to the hive to join their old family, which by now has a young queen in residence.

If the bee-keeper has few colonies and is glad to start another one, he may simply house them all in a new hive, taking care to give them a little honey to get them started. Alternatively, he may want to use the swarm to swell the numbers of a weak hive. Bees from a given colony recognize their own kind by smell and may attack and kill natives of other hives, so their keeper must somehow delude them into thinking that they are all of the same family. A time-honoured Alsace method is to mix up a little cocktail of Pernod, water and sugar. This is sprinkled onto both the swarmed bees and the family with which they are to be united. That way, all is harmony in the hive and the newly reinforced family should go from strength to strength.

The swarming season is a good moment for a new bee-keeper to get started. In his choice of hive, he will

Apis Mellifera Mellifera

be influenced both by local custom and availability, and convenience of use. Where bees are concerned, before the aspiring apiarist grate-fully accepts a wandering swarm, he might give some thought to the type of bee he would like to keep, for – like Pooh Bear – he may be con-cerned about getting "the wrong sort of bees". Many a British bee-keeper's heart swells with patriotic pride at the mention of the so-called British black bee (*Apis mellifera mellifera*), though it is also known as the French or Ger-man black, and its original homeland is all of Europe north

Apis Mellifera Ligustica

and west of the Alps. Stout and hardy, it is generally considered to be the best British bee for the worst British weather. Over the Channel down in the Gard, bee-master Monsieur Boileau – whose honey stall at the Saturday morning market in Uzès brings people from far and wide – swears by his small and slender, yellow-girdled Italian bees (*Apis mellifera ligustica*) However, as you would expect of a bee from warmer climes, the Italian bee does not take kindly to northerly winters.

From farther afield, originally from Austria and Yugoslavia, comes the dark Carniolan bee (*Apis m. carnica*),

Apis Mellifera Carnica

nowadays much favoured by Swiss, Alsatian and black Forest bee-keepers. The books describe it as a quiet and gentle character which can withstand even the hardest winters, though it has an annoying tendency to swarm. Still further east, the Caucasus are the original home of *Apis mellifera caucasica*, the long-tongued dark grey caucasian bee popularly known as the "red clover bee". New Zealand-bred bees are also a popular choice with budding bee-keepers because of their gentle ways and good breeding habits.

Mention should certainly be made of Brother Adam of Buckfast Abbey who – in a remote and inhospitable corner of Dartmoor in

Apis Mellifera Caucasica

England – has spent decades cross-breeding queens in an attempt to arrive at the perfect bee. The resulting Buckfast queens have been described by at least one

Apis Mellifera Adansonii bee expert as the Margaux of the bee world. Definitely not to be recommended is the Africanized bee, *Apis mellifera adansonii*, which was let out of its Pandora's box in Brazil in 1957. Though its reputation as a sort of Jaws of modern apiculture has long since been established by the popular press, bee-keepers throughout the American continent are by no means wholly hostile to these so-called "killer bees". Their nasty habits are more than compensated for by their high productivity.

In any case, however pure the original strain may be, the hive will soon revert to a fine pack of mongrels, probably with characteristics rather different from (and often more quarrelsome than) those of the original race. The best the aspiring apiarist can hope for is a bee which is resistant to disease, good at breeding, a hard worker prepared to go out in all weathers, an efficient little hoarder of provisions for the winter months and friendly to the neighbours.

By early summer, the novice bee-keeper will have taken his first few faltering steps (and maybe even a swarm), while the veteran will be well into his stride. In France, an old tradition has it that transhumance of bees (moving them to a prime nectar site) should take place before Midsummer's Day (*la Saint Jean*). By then, the *apiculteur* will have selected a strong, well-populated hive and carefully packed it into the back of his battered Deux Chevaux van. He sets off across country to a previously selected site, perhaps the edge of a pine forest to catch the pine honeydew or maybe beside a field of some crop which the farmer is more than happy to have pollinated. His remaining hives will be regularly checked on for their development.

Soon the extractor will be dusted down ready for the first harvest. Above all, the bee-keeper takes great care to make his extracting room completely bee-proof. Bees are as fond of honey as humans are, and once they catch a whiff of it, they may descend in droves to rob the precious food, squabbling over the spoils and stinging anyone within range. Shut away in his *cave*, sitting on an old stool, the bee-keeper dips

his large-bladed knife into hot water, then deftly slices the wax off the surface of the frames to uncap the cells and allow the honey to flow. Then the frames are put in the extractor and spun round. Out of the bottom comes the honey which is filtered, ripened and potted up in suitable containers. The bee-keeper is happy and satisfied. The first fruits of his labours are in.

Bingham uncapping knife

In July, that same swarm of bees which in an English May was worth a load of hay (and in June a silver spoon) is now not worth a fly – simply because it is too late in the season for this young family to accomplish anything useful before the winter. If there is a small swarm, the best the bee-keeper can do is to unite it with an under-populated hive. In areas where there is a worthwhile late nectar or honeydew flow, the bee-keeper may move his hives for a second time, perhaps to the moorlands for heather honey, or to the chestnut groves for the dark, intensely flavoured *miel de châtaignier*. The feast of St. Bartholomew, 24 August, is traditionally the latest date by which honey should be removed from the hives. As summer draws to a close, the main tasks of the bee-keeper are accomplished.

The time now comes for a careful check on the hive, the last chance to make sure that all is in order before shutting up shop for winter. Upper storeys are removed and frames are concentrated to reduce the space in which the colony clusters for warmth in winter. Old, darkened combs are sent off to be recycled. This is a crucial time for the bee-keeper if his hives are to be of any use next year, for the bees hatching out now will be next spring's early workers, the foundation of his families. He treats them against a number of nasty bee diseases rejoicing in sinister names such as acarine, nosema, varroa and – perhaps most alarming-sounding of all – disappearing disease. The varroa mite in particular inspires in the twentieth-century bee-keeper rather the same sort of dread that the phylloxera aphids did in the nineteenth-century wine grower, for it can wipe out whole colonies.

At around this time, too, many bee-keepers start to feed their bees a sugar or honey solution so they have sufficient stocks to take them through the winter. Alternatively, they may choose not to feed the bees at all but simply to leave them enough honey on the comb to enable them to over-winter on their own stocks.

Once the bee-keeper sees that his colonies are no longer going out to seek nectar from the few remaining flowers, it is a sign that they have eaten their fill and have enough stocks to last through the winter months. Nets may be arranged over the hives to keep away marauding blue tits or wood-peckers; a piece of fine wire netting is placed over the hive entrance to stop mice getting in. In very cold regions, the hives may be cosily covered with blankets; it makes the bee-keeper feel better, though it is doubtful if it makes any difference to the bees. Discreet little visits continue throughout the winter months, though the seasoned apiarist can tell from quiet observation of the hive entrance that all is well and knows to leave well alone. It is sufficient to make sure that the entrance is kept clear of bee corpses and other debris which might interfere with ventilation.

In the depths of winter, at least in our part of the world, the hives lie beneath a light covering of snow and all is still.

The bee-keeper busies himself with main-
tenance work and honey marketing; he may dip
his own beautifully scented beeswax candles, or
take courses with the local bee-keeping associa-
tion to find out about new developments. Once the snow-
drops start to poke their noses out of the ground and the
catkins to bloom, the queen will resume laying. The bee-
keeper's job continues to be one of quiet observation.
Sometimes he is seen around mid-day bending low, one ear
pressed to the hive. The slightest sound like the soughing of
the wind in the tops of the trees reassures him that there is
life in the old colony yet. As winter wears on, he watches for
warm sunny days when snow still lies on the ground and the
bees might be tempted to fly out joyously to greet the spring,
only to fall flat on their faces in the snow and freeze to death.
As a discouragement, he leans a tile or piece of cardboard
against the entrance to shade out the light.

One fine day in the New Year, the bees emerge (presumably in some discomfort after months of holding back) to do
their business. Great store is set by this delicately termed
Reinigungsflug ("cleansing flight"), one of the earliest signs of
life from the hive and eagerly awaited. German bee books
advise the *Bienenvater* ("bee father") to warn the neighbours
of this impending biological event, and to offer them placa-
tory pots of honey, for woe betide the unwary housewife
who may have hung out her washing on such a day. But the
bee father is happy because it is an indication that all is well
in the hive. Soon he will be busy once more with his bees,
the pollen-rich pussy willow announces the coming of spring
and soon the nectar will start to flow. The bee-keeper's year
has come full circle.

FIVE

The
PHYSICIAN IN
THE HIVE

There was an old man of Kilkenny
Who never had more than a penny,
He spent all that money
On onions and honey
That knowing old man of Kilkenny

Anon.

A whole book could be written on the health-giving and healing properties of honey and other products from the hive. Yet, while most people agree that honey is *good*, opinions on whether it is actually *good for you* are sharply divided. Harold McGee, the author of *On Food and Cooking*, who holds a science degree and a doctorate in English literature, states bluntly that "there are plenty of reasons for liking honey, but nutrition and medicinal value are not two of them." Arrayed against him is a veritable army of partisans ranging from Aristotle to Barbara Cartland. All are ready to swear blind that this natural sweetmeat is not only an essential food, but a panacea for practically all known ills. It is sometimes hard to find exactly where the truth lies.

What is honey? The *Illustrated Encyclopaedia of Beekeeping* describes it, somewhat unhelpfully, as "an extremely variable mixture of many substances". Its composition depends on a number of factors, including the plants which gave the

nectar (or honeydew), the soil on which they grew, the climate in general and the weather in particular, and not least the bees themselves. The main components are two sorts of sugar – glucose and fructose – which together make up about seventy per cent of honey. Other sugars account for about another ten per cent and the rest is water. Small quantities of acids and minerals are found, and infinitesimal amounts of vitamins.

"People who know the food value of honey", claims native Vermonter Dr. D. C. Jarvis in his book *Folk Medicine*, "are more likely to eat it regularly than those whose knowledge of it is vague." Is honey, in fact, a valuable food? The glucose and fructose which make up the better part of it are more easily assimilated by the human body than white sugar, because they have already been partially digested by the bees. This can be important for both the very young and the very old with either immature or failing digestive systems. Honey is a source of instant energy, useful for sportsmen and women who are likely to be indulging in sudden surges of activity. It is also fattening – with around eighty per cent sugar it could hardly be otherwise – a fact often conveniently overlooked by those dazzled by its health-giving image. (Gram for gram, however, it is less calorific than refined white sugar – 5 tbsp (3½oz/100g) honey contains around 300 calories, against 400 for the same amount of sugar; honeys with a high fructose content (mainly the liquid ones) also *seem* sweeter than white sugar, so in theory you should need less to get the same sweetening effect.) There is talk of an enzyme in honey which retards dental decay; on the other hand, both the fructose and the sucrose it contains are famous teeth-rotters.

The minerals contained in a given honey depend on the soil on which the honey-giving plants were grown, but potassium will certainly be present, as may sodium, calcium, magnesium, iron, copper, manganese, chlorine, phosphorus, sulphur and silica. Scientists describe the level of vitamins found in an average honey as "nutritionally insignificant"; health foodies and honey fans claim that it contains "all the vitamins needed by the human body". Both are right.

In short, honey is easily digested, it gives you energy, it can make you fat, it can rot your teeth, it has some minerals, and few vitamins.

And honey's therapeutic value? Historically speaking, for many ancient peoples who regarded honey as a gift from the gods, it was a natural step to believe that it had certain divine, almost magical, qualities. On a more practical level, one of the earliest "therapeutic" uses of honey was in conjunction with other (bitter) medicinal substances to mask their nasty taste. By far the most frequently cited medicinal use of honey in ancient times was as a healing salve in combination with some sort of grease for open wounds. The Sumerian *asu*, or physician, of the fourth milennium BC favoured pounding it to a paste with "fat from the kidney of a male sheep" and a few other exotic ingredients like myrrh and gum of aleppo pine. The result was used to make a poultice for wrapping a wounded head. Guido Majno, in his compelling book, *The Healing Hand*, quotes from the Smith papyrus ("the most ancient medical text of mankind"), in which a treatment used by the ancient Egyptians for a gash in the eyebrow is outlined: "Now after thou hast stitched it, thou shouldst bind fresh meat upon it the first day. If thou findst that the stitching of this wound is loose, thou shouldst draw it together for him. . . and thou shouldst treat it with grease and honey every day until he recovers." Honey is the standard antiseptic of the Smith papyrus: of the 900 remedies mentioned in the text, 500 contain honey.

Like his Egyptian counterparts, the Indian *vaidya* (the physician, or "he who knows") prescribed a honey and ghee paste for arrow wounds, or snake bites, or to aid the healing of pierced ears. Hippocrates was particularly partial to honey. He commended it to his patients as part of a simple diet and also, in conjunction with vinegar as a pain-killer and together with various medicinal substances for acute fevers.

It was at the top of Aristotle's list of healing substances, while Pliny was another one to recognize its value in the treatment of eye disorders. Cataracts were candidates for the honey treatment: a Roman named Vigerius reported with

evident satisfaction that he had "cured a horse stone blind with honey and salt and a little crock of a pot mixed. In less than three days, it has eaten off a tough film and the horse never complained thereafter. . ."

Theophrastus claimed to have the answer to a perennial male problem: "the water of the honeycomb or distilled honey for preventing the hair falling off and causing it to

grow." Egyptian, Greek and Roman physicians concurred on
the value of honey as a laxative; Roman doctors clearly
understood its power as a sleeping potion. They counselled
their patients against its use just before bedtime for fear they
might not be able to get up in the morning.

Frequent references are made in ancient medical texts to
the value of honey in respiratory tract problems, from

coughs and colds to bronchitis and asthmatic conditions. Galen, the first-century Greek physician and scholar, recommended it for such disorders, as did Avicenna, whose *Canon of Medicine* published 800 years later became a popular text throughout the Middle East and Europe. In the year 900, the Leech book of Glastonbury Abbey in England again invoked the therapeutic powers of honey in cases of "dimness of the eyes" (presumably cataracts), as well as for hair shortage. Throughout the Middle Ages, European doctors and apothecaries continued to testify to the efficacy of honey for any or all of the above.

With so many and such diverse claims made throughout medical history on honey's behalf, you can hardly help wondering if there was anything in them, and whether honey has any use in modern-day medicine. Drs. Zumla and Lulat, whose paper "Honey – a remedy rediscovered" was published in the *Journal of the Royal Society of Medicine* in July 1989, certainly think so. They conclude "the therapeutic potential of uncontaminated, pure honey is grossly under-utilized. It is widely available in most communities and although the mechanism of action of several of its properties remains obscure and needs further investigation, the time has now come for conventional medicine to lift the blinds off this 'traditional remedy' and give it its due recognition." Honey is included in the pharmacopoeias of Argentina, Britain, China, Egypt, France, Japan, Portugal and Spain. Martindale, "the pharmacists' bible", refers to its broad-spectrum antimicrobial action, its use in oral rehydration therapy for acute diarrhoea and its value in wound healing. There is no doubt that honey has antiseptic and antibiotic properties. The reasons for this are still improperly understood, but three factors are certainly instrumental. Firstly, honey is an acid medium and this acidity precludes and retards bacterial growth. Secondly, honey draws out moisture from its surrounding area; in the case of infection, moisture is sucked out of bacterial cells and they shrivel and die. Finally, when honey comes into contact with moisture and is diluted, an antibiotic mechanism is triggered involving hydrogen peroxide, a well-known bactericidal substance. (This is the famous "inhibine" of the 'thirties, so-called when the phenomenon was first noticed.)

Some contemporary physicians are once again waking up to the potential of this traditional remedy. Guido Majno quoted above (himself a noted professor of pathology) decided to test some of the Egyptians' theories of which he had read. He made up his own mixture of one-third honey and two-thirds fat and applied it to a wound. To his surprise, he found that the dressing on which it was applied remained moist and did not stick to the wound, while the honey itself appeared to be absorbed. He concluded that it was "harmless to tissues, aseptic, antiseptic and antibiotic" and that "in view of the technology of the Pharaonic days, it would be difficult to produce a more sensible ointment [than honey and grease]". The use of honey (with lard) for treating small wounds and ulcers during World War II is well documented. (Propolis, bee glue, was used in the same way.) A nursing friend of mine relates that in New Guinea honey is routinely and successfully used as a healing ointment. Studies carried out in hospitals in France and Britain show dramatically increased rates of post-operative healing of open wounds and formation of scar tissue when honey is used on dressings. (Sugar has about the same effect, but honey is easier to apply and draws the moisture out more effectively.)

For many of the same reasons, honey is considered to be effective in the treatment of bacteria-caused diarrhoea. In a much-quoted study, bacteriologist Dr. W. G. Sackett, of the Colorado Agricultural College, in the United States, carried out tests which proved that common gut bacteria, such as salmonella, chigella and *E. coli* simply cannot survive a concentrated onslaught of honey. It may be the same principle which prevents germs growing in your jam: if you add enough sugar, the bugs do not stand a chance.

For every scientifically tested honey-based remedy, there must be at least a dozen more which fall into what could be called the "wishful thinking" category. This certainly does not mean they do not work, only that you would have a hard job proving efficacy to the American Food and Drug Administration (FDA) or other similar organizations. For coughs, colds and fevers, people still swear by gargling with a honey and water solution, though many more prefer the old remedy of a hot toddy: honey, lemon juice, whisky and water, the proportions varying according to the patient's fondness for each of the component parts. Certainly the honey acts as a sedative and minor pain-killer, and the lemon juice contains healing vitamin C (unless you kill it by overheating it). The whisky speaks for itself. If the cold spreads to the ears, you can always try a sticky old English remedy for earache: a piece of onion dipped in honey and inserted into the ear. Another old Anglo-Saxon answer to baldness (which sounds more painful by far than the condition) was to rub a cut onion vigorously over the bald head until it was red, then to apply honey as a soothing (and sticky) salve.

Dr. Jarvis, that noted friend of honey quoted above, claimed "one of the uses to which the moisture-attracting ability of honey can be put is to attract and hold the fluid in the child's body during the hours of sleep, so that bed-wetting does not take place." He also relates that trouble-some night-time cramps in the legs are eased by a little honey at bedtime, and that a patient suffering from arthritis was completely cured once she started taking her daily dose of honey. There is a

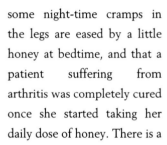

a related theory that bee-keepers seldom suffer from rheu-matism or arthritis because they are frequently stung. Some substances contained in bee stings are thought to give them protection.

The supposed therapeutic value of royal jelly deserves a brief mention. Produced by worker bees and fed exclusively to potential queens, it produces spectacular increases in weight and growth in bees. Queen bees are amazingly fertile and also live far longer than ordinary bees – four to five years (if left to their own devices), as opposed to around forty days for workers. While royal jelly is of undoubted value to bees, there is little evidence to suggest that humans need it, or indeed even benefit from it. It is nevertheless vigorously promoted as a health supplement, an aid to growth, an appetite stimulant, a mood enhancer, an aphrodisiac and

fertility booster, a wrinkle disperser and a life extender.

Perhaps the most comprehensive claims as to how (and where) honey does you good have been made by Dr. Yves Donadieu of the Faculty of Medicine in Paris, author of a book on the natural therapeutic qualities of honey, pollen, propolis and royal jelly. A summary of his suggestions for the uses of various types of honey is often handed out at point of sale in France by specialist honey marketers. Acacia honey is said to be good for the lazy bowel, while heather honey is recommended for urinary tract infections, for anaemia and general fatigue. Both eucalyptus and pine honeys help in the case of respiratory infections, as does lavender, which is also good for arthritis. Orange or linden blossom honey is indicated for the patient suffering from spasmodic or nervous conditions (including insomnia), rosemary for liver problems and digestive disorders (presumably the famous French *crise de foie* by any other name). Finally, fevers should be fed with sunflower honey.

The TASTE OF HONEY

Isn't it funny
How a bear likes honey?
Buzz, buzz buzz,
I wonder why he does?
Winnie-the-Pooh A. A. Milne 1926

Bears have always liked honey. They got there first, long before man got his sticky paws into the nest. Pooh, though by his own admission a bear of very little brain, certainly had the good sense to like honey. But A. A. Milne does not tell us what sort he liked. Perhaps being a very English kind of bear and living near Ashdown Forest, he had a fondness for fine heather honey, or flower honey made from the yellow broom, gorse and wild flowers which (I fondly imagine) flourish there.

For the honey-lover, there is a gratifyingly wide range of different honeys to choose from – as many honeys as there are *crus de vin*, claims one French author. There are single flower, multiflower, honeydew, and blended honeys. They may be creamy or runny, crystallized or deliciously crunchy and still on the comb.

Single flower honeys come, as the name suggests, principally from a single nectar source. In practice, they are seldom exclusively from one sort of flower but will have little contributions from all the flora which was available at

the time the bees were busy foraging. Have you ever
wondered how the bee-keeper keeps his pine honey separate
from, say, his lavender, rosemary or heather honey? I had

always supposed that perhaps he had a certain type of bee
which fancied only a certain sort of flower and turned its
nose up at the others. In fact, there are two explanations. In
the simplest case, the bee-keeper knows when a certain
shrub, or tree, or crop is in flower. Take the case of acacia
blossom, from the beautiful feathery-leaved *Robinia
pseudoacacia*. He watches its development in the gardens
and hedgerows within range of his hives and he checks his
honeycombs to see what the bees are bringing in. As the
acacia blossom fades, he promptly harvests the honey and
labels it accordingly. Empty combs are put into the hive
ready to be filled with the next type of nectar the bees
choose to bring in.

A more calculated way of obtaining single flower honey is
to practise migratory bee-keeping. In this case, the bee-
keeper moves some hives to the vicinity of a particular crop
with the express purpose of making honey from the nectar it
provides. This may be a field of lavender in Provence, or an
area of wild rosemary in Spain; or perhaps the bees have
been invited to the orchard of a Swiss apple farmer to ensure
cross-pollination of his Golden Delicious and Cox's Orange
Pippins. When the blossom fades, the apiarist removes the
combs, harvests the honey, puts it in containers and labels it
accordingly. The hives are taken home or moved to another
location, where the process is repeated, sometimes several
times in a given year.

Multi-flower honeys (called, for example, flower honey, or *miel des fleurs*, or *Blütenhonig* depending on where they come from) are – or should be – a delightfully rich mix of widely varying flora from all around the hive during a given period. In mixed arable and semi-cultivated countryside areas like ours in Alsace, the bees browse first among the early cherry and apple blossoms. Then, before the first hay is cropped, they forage in rough grasslands full of cornflowers, clover, dandelions, harebells and brambles. But the small-scale, mixed arable farmer of southern Alsace is a dying breed. Where once there was a rich variety of wild flowers

and a wide range of cultivated crops, excessive use of nitrates has all but wiped out the wild flowers of yesterday, while vast tracts of oilseed rape now dominate much of the northern European countryside. Country bees in these areas of huge monocultures have less choice of flowers for foraging; their so-called flower honey seems somehow one-dimensional. Town bees, ironically, have a better time of it by far. Increasingly, the best multi-flower honeys are said to come from bees which frequent bright suburban gardens and parks full to bursting with lovingly planted annuals, perennials, mixed shrubbery and tall acacias and catalpas.

Honeydew honeys are especially interesting. One sort is pine honey, *le miel de sapin* from Alsace and the Jura in France. How, I wondered aloud to my neighbour Monsieur Auguste, can the bees get nectar from the pine trees which don't seem to be in flower? There occurs, he explained, a mysterious and wonderful chain of natural events. A certain sort of plant-sucking insect (he calls it *une puce*, a flea) extracts sap from the plant and excretes it in the form of honeydew (In Alsace, pine honey is sometimes known as

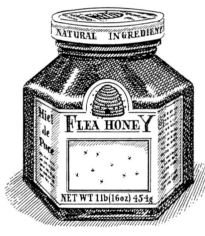

miel de puce – flea honey.) The bees recuperate the sweet secretion as if it were nectar and make it into a particularly dark and richly flavoured honey. When the honeydew stops flowing (which the bee-keeper can tell by observing the pine trees, and also from the colour of the honey in the combs) he harvests the honey. Above all he takes care to remove it from the combs before winter. Bees winter badly on honeydew honey which can give them diarrhoea; sugar solution (fed after the last honey harvest) suits their delicate digestive system better.

Then there are blended honeys, often from various parts of the world. They are put together by a honey blender who buys in bulk from many different sources. Unlike a multi-flower honey where the bee does the "blending", blended honey is mixed by a man in a white coat. It's a bit like the difference between Châteauneuf-du-Pape and Lieb-fraumilch. The former is made from up to thirteen different grape varieties fermented and vinified together to give a complex yet harmonious wine whose nature many vary from year to year. The latter is made by mixing several finished wines to give an extremely predictable beverage with a fairly neutral flavour designed to offend no-one. The objective (in the case of both blended honey and Liebraumilch) is not so much titillation of the taste buds as standardization of flavour.

Some bee-keepers prefer to market their honey by the area of origin, rather than specifying the flower(s) from which it came. This may be because the area has always been renowned for its honey, as in *miel de Narbonne*; or it may be because the bee-keeper prefers to draw a veil over the predominating local crop particularly – in Europe at least – if it is oilseed rape. Yorkshire honey, *miel du gâtinais, Schwarzwälder* or *Schweizerischer Bienenhonig* are other examples of European regionally labelled honeys.

The question is sometimes raised as to what happens if bees forage from polluted or even from poisonous flowers. In classical times, honey from the Pontic region of Turkey was renowned for its toxic effect, thought to be due to nectar from a certain rhododendron. Isolated cases of honey poisoning still occur but they are extremely rare. Bees are highly sensitive to pollution and are used (notably around Los Alamos in New Mexico) as monitors of the atmosphere. They have also been used experimentally by mining concerns as mineral prospectors: the composition of their honey serves as an indicator of the mineral levels in the soils in a given area. However, even if honey in the hive contains small amounts of toxins, once it is ripe and on sale, these will have disappeared. Severe pollution or large toxic doses of insecticides or pesticides will kill off the bees long before there is any chance of the product being poisoned.

Finally, the consistency of honey varies enormously. Many people wonder why some honeys are liquid, while others set smoothly, or granulate rather crunchily. They suppose vaguely that the "manufacturer" has done something to influence the texture. Quite right: the bee ("the manufacturer") influences the consistency of honey by the choice of plants from which it forages. The amateur bee-keeper's product will be as nature intended it: sometimes liquid, sometimes solid, sometimes somewhere in between. If an industrial honey processor comes into the picture, things are a bit different. He can modify the natural consistency of the product by the various industrial processes he uses.

Honey, as made by the bees and when first removed from the comb, is liquid. This is because it is warm – the hive temperature hovers around a fairly steamy 96°F (35°C). Once the honey cools it reacts differently depending on what sort it is. Some honeys, such as acacia blossom and tupelo, are naturally runny and tend to stay so almost indefinitely. Others, notably oilseed rape and dandelion, crystallize (or granulate) very rapidly. Left to their own devices, most honeys start life fairly liquid and gradually granulate. (Honey can always be re-liquefied by placing it in a bain-marie and gently heating it until the crystals dissolve.)

On an industrial level, bulk honey processors keep their honey liquid by flash heating it to dissolve any crystals, and by rigorously filtering out "impurities", such as protein-rich specks of pollen, upon which crystals might grow. Alternatively, if solid honey is required, a liquid honey is "seeded" with very fine crystals so the resulting granulation is fine and even.

Comb honey (formerly known as card honey or section honey) is a special case. Very fine, unwired wax foundation set within a wooden or plastic square or round frame is provided in the hive for the bees to furnish directly with honey. In the days when adulteration of honey was commonplace and before effective tests to detect it had been developed, comb honey was much more commonly found. Sadly, it is becoming rare. It is expensive and fiddly for bee-keepers to make, though it is the ideal way to deal with ling heather honey which because of its gelatinous consistency cannot be extracted from the honeycombs with the usual machinery.

Cut comb honey is an easier way of arriving at the same result as comb honey: instead of putting round or square frames into the hive for the bees to work on directly, a thin, unwired sheet of wax foundation is placed in a normal frame. Once filled with honey, the bee-keeper cuts out sections which are then either placed in wooden or plastic frames, or wrapped in cellophane. The sections may also be used to make so-called chunk honey, where a piece of honeycomb is suspended in a jar of liquid honey. It is important to choose honeys which stay liquid, such as mountain sage from California, tupelo from Florida, orange blossom or gallberry otherwise the visual effect is lost.

What does honey taste of? Though it is basically made up of different sorts of sugar, honey is a complex product with many different aromas and flavours: at a recent count, 181 substances have been identified in honey. Some of the things which influence its flavour are the plants principally visited by the bees to get nectar (or honeydew), the soil on which they grew, the timing both of nectar collection by the bees and the harvesting of the honey by the bee-keeper. On top of these measurable factors come the unmeasurable ones: taste is a highly subjective matter and what is absolute heaven to one honey-taster may be utter horror to another.

Eva Crane in her *Book of Honey* suggests that a good start in getting to grips with the taste of honey is to learn to identify ten fairly commonly encountered examples: acacia, oilseed rape, rosemary, orange, lime (linden or basswood), sweet chestnut, thyme, eucalyptus, bell heather and ling heather. They range in intensity of flavour from mild to strong and in colour and consistency from water-white and runny to dark, almost wine-coloured and oddly gelatinous.

Acacia is sometimes considered the aristocrat of honeys, a fact reflected in its high price. Very pale and clear, some people find in it some of the delicate aromas and flavours of acacia blossom. It is one of the sweetest honeys, due in part to its high fructose content (on a sweetness scale where sucrose – white sugar – is 100, fructose rates 162). Though fairly widely produced throughout continental Europe, it is most at home in eastern Europe and particularly Hungary where it is the chief source of commercially produced honey.

Oilseed rape is a difficult one to identify, mainly because – at least in Europe – it is seldom labelled as such because the consumer is apt to be a bit sniffy about it. Nevertheless, it is very widely produced: because of modern agricultural methods most rural bee-keepers throughout Europe rely on this crop for the bulk of their early honey harvest. Bees love it and travel long distances for the nectar and pollen it contains in profusion. It makes a pale, straw-coloured honey which crystallizes extremely quickly and very finely. It appeals to those who like a mild, creamy breakfast spread. Others find it bland, uninteresting and overly sweet. Some even detect "cabbagy" flavours in it – as rape is a brassica.

The pale amber honey made from rosemary is traditionally used in the Spanish sweet *turrón*. Though principally associated with Spain, it is found throughout the Mediterranean area and in northern Africa. Its fine, delicately herbal flavour is best appreciated when spread on bread or toast – it's almost a pity to use it in cooking.

Eucalyptus is native to Australia and is one of its major honey plants, especially in karri forest areas. It has been successfully exported to a number of European countries including Portugal, Spain, France and Italy. Given the very diverse range of eucalyptus plants, the honey varies widely, too. Mine is fairly liquid, and slow to granulate, with a rich gold-brown colour. Do not expect it to smell or taste of Vick's vapour rub; mercifully, it does not. To me, it suggests lovely complex smells of leather and beeswax. I like its slightly bitter finish.

Everyone seems to agree that orange blossom honey is delicious. It comes, as you would expect, from areas famous for their citrus crops: Spain, the U.S., especially Florida, and Israel. Uncapping a good jar of orange blossom honey is like wandering into an orange grove in full bloom. Almost overpowering citrus aromas emerge, and the taste is satisfyingly orange flavoured. The honey is pale golden and rather runny.

I vividly remember wandering around the ramparts of the town of Laon in central France one early summer's evening, assaulted on all sides by the heady perfume of the lime trees. The honey from this tree, which varies in colour from pale greenish yellow to rich golden, evokes strongly the exotic smell of the tree in flower; the flavour is almost minty and very pronounced. Its texture is fairly finely crystallized and like eucalyptus, it has a slightly bitter finish.

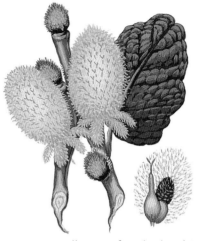

Chestnut honey, very commonly found in northern Italy and Ticino, leaves no-one indifferent: either you love it or you hate it. It is dark brown and usually quite runny. Its taste has been variously described as penetrating, tannic and astringent.

When it became known that I was working on this book, a colleague of my husband's in their Greek company staggered into head office one day bearing an 11lb (5kg) drum of thyme honey from the Pelopponese. It is ambrosial: rich, golden, a little clouded with tiny specks of pollen and other "impurities" which would doubtless have been chased out by an over-zealous processor. It has been a constant companion at the breakfast table and has enlivened most of the dishes tested in the recipe chapter.

Heather honey is the last and by no means least in this introduction to honeys. Most people, when talking of heather honey, mean the honey from ling heather (*calluna vulgaris*), characterized by its gelatinous consistency which makes it a good candidate for selling in the comb – it doesn't run about in an undisciplined sort of way. The colour ranges from a rich reddish brown to a deep amber, and it has a curious, quite distinctive (and unforgettable) bitter-sweet

flavour. Bell heather (*erica cinerea*) gives an almost port wine-coloured liquid honey which can be extracted in the normal way.

To venture into further descriptions of the world's honeys runs the risk of sounding like a honey salesman's catalogue.

To Eva Crane's Top Ten, however, I would add a couple of personal favourites, as well as some transatlantic samples, and, finally, a honey which I have never tasted but which should clearly not be missed by the honey freak. My first is the so-called *miel de puce*, the honeydew honey from the woods I survey from my kitchen window. Dark brown with almost greenish reflections in its  liquid depths, it has the characteristically pungent, minerally flavour of honeydew honeys, ever so slightly reminiscent of cough mixture. You feel it *must* be doing you good. My neighbour Monsieur Auguste pots it up at the end of the summer, complete with little specks of pollen. On the pot is a message saying that honey, being a NATURAL product, tends to crystallize, the remedy for which is to put it in a bain-marie of not more than 126°F (50°C). It is a northerly honey which cheers and braces me through the dark winter months. To lighten the mood, I like Monsieur Boileau's *miel de garrigue* from Uzès down near Nîmes. It brings the warmth of the south and reminds me of the pungent smells of the sun-baked scrub and the sounds of the crickets in the Gard.

I was especially happy to treat my sheltered European palate to a taste of three honeys for which the U.S. is renowned: tupelo, gleaned from various species of the *Nyssa* trees which line the Apalachicola River in Western Florida; sage, from bees feeding on the many different salvia plants prevalent particularly in California; and buckwheat, which intrigued me ever since I spotted an advertisement in *The Speedy Bee* (a bee-keeper's newspaper published in Georgia in the U.S.) for "pure buckwheat honey, thick, dark and stinky." Thick and dark it certainly is, but stinky is definitely unkind. (The bee-keeper is not alone in his views: my French honey tasting book attributes to it "heavy and very vulgar aromas" and labels it "persistent and detestable".) My sample (guaranteed raw, unfiltered, uncooked) is stunning with a rich, malted flavour and good acidity. I like strong honeys. The tupelo and sage are both pale golden and very runny, candidates for one of those swizzle-stick style honey dippers. The tupelo is special: very aromatic and long-lasting. The sage is nicely herbal, a little milder but still memorable.

The final one, which I shall certainly try if I ever get the chance, is the *miele amaro di Corbezzolo* from Sardinia, made from the strawberry tree (*arbutus*). It produces a honey which was said to be a particular favourite of the Marquis de Sade. It seems that certain sado-masochistic tendencies would be a prerequisite for sampling this unique honey, distinguished by an almost intolerable bitterness.

From this it will be clear that the tastes of honey are almost boundless. When you are at home, seek out a good source and sample as many as you can. When you are on your travels, make a point of picking up some local honeys to take home. When you uncap the jar in deepest winter, you will be reminded of the citrus groves of Spain, or the thyme-clad hills of Greece, the sombre pine trees of the Black Forest, or the fragrant sage bushes of southern California. Best of all, find a bee-keeper and ask him about his bees, his hives, his honey, his environment. Few people enjoy the chance to talk about their hobby (or profession) more than bee-keepers. And find time to bless him, and his bees, and *le bon Dieu* for this miraculous little product of nature.

I eat my peas with honey,
I've done it all my life,
It makes the peas taste funny,
But it keeps them on the knife.

Anon.

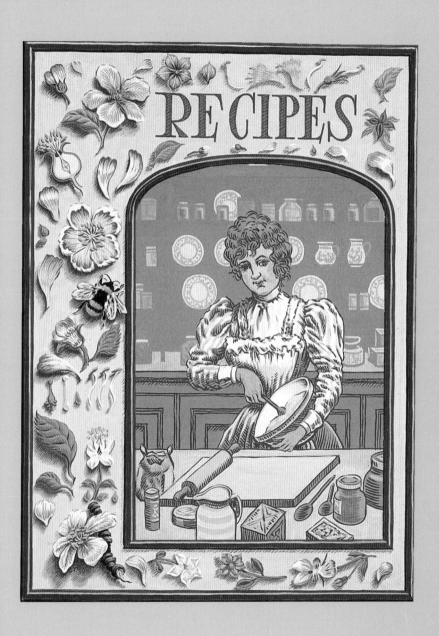

oney is a special food with a fine range of flavours. It is a pity to use it in cooking if all you want is a vague sweetening effect: you might as well use sugar which is cheaper. My aim in developing these recipes has been to allow the honey to speak for itself, and not just to get swallowed up in the crowd. Types of honey are rarely specified for a particular recipe, because not all honeys are available everywhere. Make your own experiments depending on what you have.

When adding honey to a sauce, always add it at the end after any reducing has been done: if honey is too violently heated, its complex aromas are lost and it may burn. In desserts, neutral-tasting foods like cream, eggs or natural yogurts make a good backdrop. Honey can be used to replace sugar in any of your favourite cake recipes. (As W. T. Fernie commented in his delightful book *Meals Medicinal*, published in 1905: "a plain cake of currants or seed, made with Honey in place of sugar, is a pleasing addition to the tea-table, and a useful preventive of constipation.")

As honey is generally sweeter than sugar, allow 1 measure of honey for 1¼ sugar. It also contains more water so you may need less liquid: add it carefully and stop when the mixture is the right consistency. Because honey is hygroscopic, it keeps breads and cakes nicely moist.

Creamy Honey and Herb Salad Dressing

A nicely piquant, fairly thick dressing in which you can ring the changes with different mustards, oils, vinegars and honeys.

Makes 2¼ cups (18 oz/500ml)

1 tsp salt
pepper
1 tsp mustard
1¼ cups (10 oz/300ml) oil
7 tbsp vinegar or lemon or lime juice
2 tsp honey
2 tbsp natural yogurt or 1 egg
fresh herbs in season, to taste

Blend the ingredients together until quite smooth and emulsified. Add a little water if necessary to thin out the dressing. Keep in the refrigerator, covered.

Warm Duck Salad with Honey Vinegar

In Alsace, we have a product known as Melfor, a vinegar made with the addition of honey and herbs. Here it is used to deglaze the pan in which the strips of duck have been fried before they are tossed over the dressed salad leaves.

Serves 4

salad leaves (cos, oakleaf, rocket)
dressing (page 87)
12 cherry tomatoes
8oz (250g) duck breast
salt and pepper
1 tsp oil
3tbsp Melfor or wine vinegar
1 tbsp honey

Toss the salad in the dressing and arrange on 4 plates. Halve the cherry tomatoes and arrange on top of the salad leaves.

Skin the duck breast, cut in thin strips and season. Sear in hot oil in a heavy-based pan and scatter over the salads.

Beat the vinegar and honey briefly into the pan juices, stirring well to scrape up any bits on the bottom of the pan. Pour the mixture over the salads and serve at once.

Marinated Shrimp or Scampi with Honey and Ginger

There is a pleasing clash of hot-sweet flavours in this finger-licking dish with its oriental overtones. Raw shrimp or scampi give a more succulent result than ready cooked ones. Serve with rice with a cubed avocado stirred in.

Serves 2 for a rather special supper, 4 for a first course

salt and freshly ground black pepper
small knob fresh ginger root grated, or ¹/₂ tsp ground
3 tbsp dry white wine
1 tbsp soy sauce
1 tbsp honey
20 giant shrimp or scampi, shelled
1 tbsp oil

In a bowl, mix together the salt, pepper, ginger, wine, soy sauce and honey. Add the shellfish, turn to coat well and marinate several hours or overnight in the refrigerator.

Lift the shellfish out of the marinade and fry in hot oil, stirring, for 3–4 minutes, until pink. (Or, put in a microwave-safe dish, cover with plastic wrap (cling film) and microwave on High for 2 minutes, stirring halfway through.)

The marinade can either be boiled down to a syrupy consistency and added to a little mayonnaise to eat with the shrimp or scampi, or used as part of the liquid for cooking the rice.

Fish and Leeks with Red Butter Sauce

A dish with a beautiful contrast of colours and a fine combination of flavours: white fish on a bed of vibrant green leeks surrounded by a red wine butter sauce enriched with honey. This is a last-minute affair, best kept for an elegant little supper (or fairly substantial first course) for friends in the kitchen.

Serves 4

4 fillets of firm white fish, such as sole or turbot,
each about 5oz (150g)
salt and pepper
juice of 1/2 lemon
7 tbsp fish stock
5 tbsp dry white wine
5 tbsp (2 1/2oz/75g) butter
4 small leeks, trimmed, finely sliced and well rinsed
1/4 bottle red wine
2 tbsp honey

Season the fish, put in a buttered ovenproof dish with the lemon juice stock, white wine and 4–5 small dots of butter. Cover with foil and bake at 300°F/150°C/Gas Mark 2 for about 8 minutes or until just opaque.

Meanwhile, put the leeks in a pan with 6 tbsp water and another knob of butter. Cook briskly until barely tender, about 10 minutes. Drain well and keep warm.

Lift fish out of its juices and keep it warm. Boil the juices in a wide pan with the red wine until reduced to about a teacupful. Off the heat, beat in the remaining butter and the honey with a wire whisk. Season to taste.

Put a little bed of leek on each heated plate, a fish fillet on top and some sauce around.

Alternatively, to prepare in a microwave, cook the fish in a microwave-safe dish covered with plastic wrap (cling film) on high for about 4 minutes, rearranging half way through. Cook the leeks, covered, for about 4 minutes, stirring half way through. Make sauce as above.

Carrot "Fettucine" with Noodles

A delicate vegetarian dish of honeyed and spiced carrots cut in thin strands and tossed with the noodles. Serve with plenty of grated Parmesan cheese, or without cheese as an accompanying vegetable. *Paglia e fieno* are thin green and white ribbon noodles, made with spinach and egg.

Serves 4

1¼lb (600g) carrots
¼ cup (2oz/50g) butter
3 tbsp water
salt
a small knob fresh ginger root, grated, or ½ tsp ground
2 tsp honey
juice of ½ orange
4–5 tbsp heavy (double) cream or crème fraîche
1lb 2oz (500g) thin noodles or paglia e fieno

Peel thin fettucine-like strands off the carrots with a vegetable peeler, leaving the yellow woody centres behind.

Cook the carrots in a wide pan with the butter, water, salt, ginger honey and juice over moderate heat for 5–6 minutes, or until the water is evaporated and the carrots barely tender. Stir in the cream.

Meanwhile, boil the pasta until just al dente, then drain, return to the pan. Toss the carrots in with the pasta.

Pan-fried Fish with Honey and Lime

A quickly prepared dish of strips of assorted fish (include some salmon for colour) with just a suspicion of honey in the sauce. For a main course, serve with fresh pasta (*paglia e fieno* looks nice) and (zucchini) courgettes.

Serves 4 for a main course, 6 for a first course

thinly pared peel (zest) and juice of lime
2lb (900g) assorted fish fillets
salt and pepper
2 tbsp (1oz/25g) butter
1¼ cups (10 oz/300ml) light (single) or whipping cream
2 tbsp honey

Cut the peel (zest) in needle-like strips, then blanch it and refresh in cold water. Cut the fish in strips. Season lightly and toss over high heat in the hot butter in a non-stick skillet (frying pan) 3–4 minutes, until just opaque. Set aside and keep warm. Beat the lime juice and cream into the pan juices with a wire whisk and simmer 4–5 minutes, stirring occasionally. Off the heat, beat in the honey with a wire whisk and stir in the lime peel (zest). Return the fish to the pan to heat through.

Roasted Monkfish with Honey and Spices

Monkfish is so wonderfully firm that it can be roasted just like a piece of meat. Here the tail is spread with a mixture of honey and spices and then roasted fairly briefly. Serve with buttered leeks or spinach, and new potatoes.

Serves 6

1 monkfish tail about 2lb 4oz (1kg)
salt and pepper
2 tbsp honey
juice of 1 lime
1 tbsp oil
1 tsp coriander seeds, crushed
1 tsp curry powder
scant 1 cup (7 oz/200ml) dry white wine
scant 1 cup (7 oz/200ml) light (single) or whipping cream

Remove the skin and any membrane from the monkfish tail. Rub the salt and pepper into it.

Mix together the honey, lime juice, oil and spices and pour the mixture over the fish. Cover with plastic wrap (cling film) and leave to marinate for a few hours in the refrigerator, turning over once or twice

Preheat the oven to 400°F (200°C, Gas Mark 6).

Roast the monkfish for about 20 minutes or until the flesh is firm to the touch and opaque. Remove and keep warm.

Tip the cooking juices into a wide pan, add the wine and boil until reduced by half. Add the cream and reduce again by half. Check the seasoning.

Cut the 2 fillets off the bone and slice them into medallions. Serve over the sauce.

Marinated Chicken Pieces

Chicken pieces are bathed overnight in a marinade then grilled (or barbecued). Serve with risotto or new potatoes.

Serves 4–6

1 chicken, about 4¹/₂lb (2kg) or 6 chicken legs
salt and pepper
3 tbsp honey
2 tbsp soy sauce
2 tsp coriander seeds, crushed
1 packet powdered saffron, or 10 saffron threads
1 onion, chopped
1 large tomato, chopped
1 tsp salt
juice of 1 lime
¼ cup (2oz/50g) butter

Cut a whole chicken into 6 pieces. Put the pieces in a shallow dish and season well.

Blend or process together the honey, soy sauce, coriander seeds, saffron, onion, tomato and salt. Spread this mixture over the chicken pieces and leave to marinate for at least 6 hours, or overnight, in a cool place.

Lift the pieces out of the marinade and broil (grill) or barbecue them, turning regularly until cooked through and the juices run clear if tested with the tip of a knife. Strain the marinade into a pan with the lime juice. Heat to boiling, then remove from the heat and beat in the butter bit by bit with a wire whisk to thicken and enrich the sauce.

Honey-Roasted Chicken with Tarragon and Lemon

By coating a chicken, guinea fowl, pheasant or turkey with a fragrant mixture of honey, lemon and oil, you get a golden, crusty skin with all the moisture conserved. Serve with roast potatoes, or *Rösti* and plenty of salad.

This is also delicious cold; skip the sauce and stir the jellied juices into a bowl of good mayonnaise.

Serves 4–6

1 chicken, about 4½lb (2kg)
salt and pepper
juice of 1 lemon
3 tbsp olive oil
1 tbsp honey
2–3 sprigs fresh tarragon, or 1 tsp dried
1 cup (8fl oz/250 ml) chicken stock
4 tbsp heavy (double) cream

Preheat the oven to 400°F (200°C/Gas Mark 6).

Rub the chicken well with salt and pepper. Beat together, with a wire whisk, the lemon juice, oil and honey as if making a vinaigrette. Pour this mixture over the bird and put some tarragon inside. Put it in a roasting pan, pour in about 6 tbsp water and roast for about 1 hour, or until golden brown and thoroughly cooked; stick a skewer into the fattest part of a leg to see if the juices run clear. Remove the bird and keep it warm.

Stir the stock into the juices in the pan and bring to the boil, stirring and scraping well. Reduce by about half, then whisk in the cream.

Spiced Shoulder of Lamb with Prunes

The accent here is north African: cinnamon, coriander, ginger and honey are rubbed into a boned and rolled shoulder of lamb before gentle roasting, then prunes are added shortly before the end. Serve with couscous or rice, and broccoli.

Serves 4–6

12 prunes
salt and pepper
1/2 tsp ground cinnamon
1 tsp coriander seeds, crushed
1/2 tsp ground ginger
2 tbsp honey
1 boned and rolled shoulder of lamb about 2 1/2lb (1.1 kg)
1 onion, chopped
1 clove garlic, crushed
1 tbsp oil

Soak the prunes in water overnight. Rub the salt, pepper, spices and honey into the lamb and leave overnight in the refrigerator for the flavours to penetrate.

Preheat the oven to 300°F (150°C/Gas Mark 2).

Soften the onion and garlic in the oil without allowing them to brown. Put them in a roasting pan or gratin dish. Put the lamb on top and add about 6 tbsp water. Roast, uncovered, for about 1 1/2 hours, until brown and tender.

Discard strings and slice meat quite thickly. Put it back in the pan with the drained prunes, return to the oven and cook for 15–20 minutes more.

Duck Breasts with Sweet-Sour Marinade

Best of all on the barbecue, but a broiler (grill) works well, too. Serve with ribbon noodles mixed with matchstick strips of lightly cooked zucchini (courgettes).

Serves 2

salt and pepper
2 small duck breasts
2 tbsp honey
1 tbsp wine vinegar or Melfor
1 tsp soy sauce
a walnut-sized piece fresh ginger root, grated
juice of 1 orange
¼ cup (2 oz/50g) butter

Rub the salt and pepper well into the duck breasts. In a shallow dish, mix together the honey, vinegar, soy sauce, ginger root and orange juice. Roll the duck breasts in the marinade and put in the refrigerator for a few hours or overnight, turning the duck breast occasionally. Light the barbecue coals or preheat the broiler (grill), and grill the breasts for 6–7 minutes on each side, or until the skin is crusty and the flesh still slightly pink. Put the marinade in a pan and boil to reduce to a syrup: take care it does not burn. Remove from the heat, beat in the butter and serve with the breasts.

Mustard-and-Honey-Glazed Ham or Pork in Pastry

This preparation can be done a day or two ahead and the meat refrigerated ready for baking. Serve with a creamy gratin of spinach.

Serves 4

2 tbsp coarse-grained mustard
1 tbsp honey
1¾lb (800g) boneless ham or smoked pork loin
10oz (300g) piecrust dough (short-crust) or puff pastry dough
1 egg, beaten with a pinch of salt

Mix together the mustard and honey and spread it over the meat. Roll out the pastry dough to a rectangle. Place the meat at one end, wet the pastry edges, bring the pastry dough up and over to encase snugly, pressing the edges well to seal. Use any trimmings to decorate. Refrigerate the meat if not baking immediately.

Preheat the oven to 400°F (200°C/Gas Mark 6).

Brush the pastry dough with egg wash, then bake for about 40 minutes, or until the pastry is golden and the meat hot through. A skewer inserted in the middle should feel rather warm to the cheek.

Spicy Game Stew

Apicius, in his Roman cook book, gives several recipes for game, of which this is an interpretation, lavishly seasoned and spiced and sweetened with honey. The latter not only softens the slightly aggressive flavour of the game and the marinade, but also (especially if you use a dark honey like pine) adds interest. Serve with *spätzle* or some creamily mashed potatoes to mop up the juices.

Serves 4–6

2lb 2oz (1kg) boneless stewing game such as venison, wild boar, hare
salt and pepper
3 fingernail-sized pieces
orange peel (zest)
1 tsp crushed coriander seeds
scant 1 cup (7 oz/200ml) red wine
1 bay leaf
1 shallot, finely chopped
1 clove garlic, crushed
2 carrots, sliced
pinch cumin seeds
flour
2 tbsp oil
scant 1 cup (200ml/7 oz) beef stock
1 tbsp honey

Trim the meat and cut it in bite-sized pieces. Put it in a non-metallic container with the salt, pepper, orange peel (zest), coriander seeds, wine, bay leaf, shallot, garlic and cumin seeds. Leave to marinate for several hours or overnight in the refrigerator, stirring the meat occasionally. Strain the meat and set aside the shallot, carrots, garlic and bay leaf; reserve the marinade.

Preheat the oven to 300°F (150°C/Gas Mark 2).

Toss the meat in flour in a plastic bag. Heat the oil in a heavy-based skillet (frying pan) and sear the meat in several batches until brown and crusty. Put the meat in a casserole as it is ready. In the same pan, soften the shallot, carrots and garlic. Add them to the casserole with the reserved marinade, the bay leaf and the stock; the meat should be barely covered. Cover with foil and a lid and braise for about 1 hour, or until the meat is tender. Stir in the honey and cook for 10 minutes more.

Calf's Liver Saute with a Sweet-Sour Finish

In this excellent dish for liver-lovers, which can also be adapted for kidneys, a splash of aromatic honey at the end provides a nice foil to the slight bitterness of variety meat (offal). Grated zucchine (courgettes) tossed in butter with garlic and shallot, and a dish of creamy yellow polenta or saffron risotto go well with it.

Serves 2

2 slices calf's liver (about 12oz (350g))
salt and pepper
3 tbsp flour
¼ cup (2oz/50g) butter
1 tsp oil
3 tbsp wine or honey vinegar
1 tbsp honey
1–2 tbsp water

Cut the liver in thin strips and season well. Shortly before frying, toss the liver strips in the flour in a plastic bag. Shake off excess flour in a colander. Heat half the butter and the oil in a heavy-based skillet (frying pan), and fry the liver over moderately high heat for 4–5 minutes, stirring and tossing, until lightly crusted but still pink inside. Remove from the pan and keep warm.

Deglaze the pan with the vinegar and reduce to about 1 tbsp. Off the heat, beat in the honey and the remaining butter with a wire whisk. If necessary, loosen the sauce with a little water. Return the liver briefly to the pan and stir it into the sauce.

Honey Crêpes

A special batter which gives a particularly light, golden crêpe with a delicate honey flavour. It can be used whenever sweet crêpes are required.

To make crêpe ice cream baskets, line an ovenproof tea-cup with them and bake at 400°F (200°C/Gas Mark 6) until golden and crisp (about 10 minutes). Enough for about 16 crêpes, 8in. (20cm) in diameter.

Serves 4

½ cup (4fl oz/125ml) water
½ cup (4fl oz/125ml) milk
1 cup (3½oz/100g) flour
2 tbsp oil
½ tsp salt
2 eggs
1 tbsp honey

Beat or process together all the ingredients to a smooth batter. Leave to rest for at least 1 hour. Beat again briefly before using.

Brush a heavy-based 8in (20cm) skillet (frying pan) with a little oil and heat. Pour in enough batter to just coat the bottom of the pan; there should be a protesting sizzle as it goes in and any excess swilling about should be immediately tipped back into the batter bowl.

Cook until the underside is golden then turn or flip to cook the other side. If you don't get about 16 crêpes, you are making them too thick. Stack up as they are ready.

Apple Pastries with Honey Sauce

In this last-minute (but infinitely worthwhile) dessert, apple slices are tossed in honey and batter and layered with brik pastry leaves or very thin crêpes. Serve with quenelles of real (spotty) vanilla ice cream or honey parfait. Brik pastry leaves are like superfine crêpes, native to north Africa and used in both sweet and salty (savoury) dishes.

Serves 4 liberally or 8 lightly

4 dessert apples, such as Cox's
¼ cup (2oz/50g) butter
2 tsp ground cinnamon
juice of ½ lemon
3 tbsp well-flavoured honey
8 brik pastry leaves or crêpes (page 103)
6 tbsp crème fraîche or heavy (double) cream

Peel, core and halve apples, then slice thinly. Fry gently in 1 tbsp (½oz/15g) butter with cinnamon, lemon juice and 1 tbsp honey until golden, turning once.

Preheat the oven to 400°F (200°C/Gas Mark 6).

Melt remaining butter. Remove interleaving papers from the brik leaves. Cut them or the crêpes in quarters. Brush the brik or crêpes with melted butter. Spread them out on

cookie (baking) sheets and bake for 10 minutes or until golden and crisp.

Alternate 4 brik or crêpe quarters with 3 apple layers, reheating briefly in the oven if necessary to crisp them up. Heat the remaining honey with the cream and drizzle some over each "cake". Serve 1 or 2 per person.

Honey Piecrust Dough
(Shortcrust Pastry)

An all-purpose sweet pastry dough which can be used in any fruit pie or cheesecake recipe. The more aromatic the honey used, the more interesting the baked pastry will be.

Makes about 10oz (300g) pastry dough

1¾ cups (7oz/200g) flour
½ tsp salt
¼ cup (2oz/50g) butter
¼ cup (2oz/50g) margarine, shortening or lard
1 tbsp runny honey
1 egg
chilled water

Cut or rub together the flour, salt, butter and margarine or lard until roughly mixed. Mix together the honey and egg and add to the flour. Add enough chilled water to make it come together into more or less of a ball. Push the result (it will look quite ragged) down a marble slab or board with the heel of your hand to blend in the fat. Gather it up into a ball, wrap in foil and chill for at least 30 minutes before using.

Apple Tart

An open-faced apple tart with a creamy custard made from yogurt, honey and eggs and perfumed with lemon peel (zest). This is just as delicious made with pears. Honey ice cream or parfait (page 109) makes a nice accompaniment, if served as a dessert rather than for tea or with coffee.

Serves 4–6

1 quantity honey piecrust dough (Shortcrust pastry) (page 106)
2–3 tbsp ground almonds or hazelnuts
4–5 dessert apples, peeled, quartered, cored and thinly sliced
3 eggs
8oz (250g) natural yogurt
2 tbsp honey
grated peel (zest) and juice of 1 lemon
confectioners' (icing) sugar

Preheat the oven to 400°F (200°C/Gas Mark 6).

Roll out the pastry dough rather thinly and line a 10-in (25cm) quiche pan with a removable base. Sprinkle the ground nuts in the bottom. Arrange the apple slices in concentric circles on top. Beat or process together the eggs, yogurt, honey, lemon peel (zest) and juice. Pour it over the fruit.

Bake for 35–40 minutes, or until nicely golden and the custard set. Cool on a rack, sprinkle with confectioners' (icing) sugar and serve at room temperature.

Honey Parfait

This is my favourite dessert in the book, and certainly the simplest: a soft ice cream with a pronounced honey flavour, which needs no stirring during the freezing. Pour it into a bread pan (loaf tin) lined with plastic wrap (cling film) freeze and cut it in slices to serve; or freeze in ramekins or yogurt pots and turn it out for serving. A fruit coulis (page 113) or an orange salad (page 111) goes well.

Serves 4–6

3 egg yolks
1 egg
½ cup (6oz/175g) honey
1¼ cups (½ pint/300ml) heavy (double) or whipping cream
3 tbsp chopped walnuts (optional)

Beat together the yolks, egg and honey with an electric mixer until thoroughly light and fluffy. Beat the cream to soft peaks, then fold it in. Stir in the walnuts if using them and freeze the parfait in the chosen container.

Greek Honey and Yogurt Tart

A recipe from Ciba-Geigy's excellent publication, *Bienenstich*, for bee-keepers the world over. It is best of all if made with the incomparable Greek thyme honey, though any well-flavoured honey will do. Greek yogurt is thicker and creamier than natural yogurt. If you can not find it, substitute quark from Germany, or any other lowfat soft cheese. A bowl of fresh raspberries served as accompaniment does not come amiss.

Serves 6

*7oz (200g) Honey piecrust dough
(Shortcrust pastry) or puff pastry
1 egg white
1lb (450g) Greek yogurt or quark
1/3 cup (4¹/₂oz/125g) honey
pinch salt
2 tsp lemon juice
3 eggs
¹/₂ tsp ground cinnamon*

Preheat the oven to 400°F (200°C/Gas Mark 6).

Roll out the pastry dough thinly and line a 10-in (26-cm) quiche pan with a removable base. Brush with egg white and chill while you prepare the filling. Beat or blend together the yogurt or quark, honey, salt, lemon juice, eggs and cinnamon until smooth. Pour into the prepared pastry case and bake for 15 minutes. Reduce the heat to 325°F (170°C/Gas Mark 3) and bake a further 30 minutes. Leave to cool in the turned off oven. Chill when cool.

Orange Salad with Honey and Nuts

The oranges are pared of peel (zest), the segments removed from their pithy case, then bathed in a mixture of orange and lemon juices with a little honey. Walnuts give added texture and interest. Serve this salad arranged around a slice of honey parfait (page 109) or for an energy-giving breakfast.

Serves 4–6

8 oranges
1 lemon
2 tbsp honey
2–3 tbsp roughly chopped walnuts

Cut the peel off 6 of the oranges with a very sharp knife, making sure no pith remains on the outside. Cut the segments out of the casing. Squeeze out any juice from the peel into a bowl. Squeeze the remaining juice from 2 oranges and the lemon.

Beat in the honey. Bathe the orange segments in the juice and chill the salad well. Sprinkle with chopped walnuts just before serving.

The Merchant Taylor's Lavender and Honey Ice Cream

This recipe for a delicate summer ice cream was given me by Simon Fooks, chef at the Merchant Taylor's Livery Company in the City of London. You may, if you wish, add crystallized lavender flowers to the mixture before freezing, for added texture.

Serves 6–8

2½ cups (1 pint/600ml) milk
vanilla bean (pod), split
3oz (90g) lavender flowers, fresh or dried, tied in a cheesecloth (muslin) bag
scant ½ cup (3oz/90g) sugar
2½ tbsp clear honey
3 egg yolks
⅔ cup (5 oz/150ml) heavy (double) cream

Scald the milk, add the vanilla bean (pod) and the lavender bag and leave to infuse for 10 minutes. Remove the vanilla and the bag.

Beat together the sugar, honey and egg yolks, add the milk, beating well to blend thoroughly. Heat the custard in a heavy-based saucepan or in a double boiler over moderate heat until it coats the back of a wooden spoon and wisps of steam appear. Do not boil.

Strain the mixture through a fine strainer (sieve) and leave to cool. Stir in the cream and freeze, stirring up once or twice to prevent ice crystals forming.

Honey Caramel Creams with Fruit Coulis

Honey is used both in the caramel and in the custard for these delicate creams. A lovely dessert served with a coulis of red summer fruits.

Serves 8

2½ tbsp honey
¼ cup (2oz/50g) sugar
4 eggs
½ cup (6oz/175g) honey
2 cups (16 oz/450ml) milk
Fruit Coulis: 1lb (450g) red fruit, such as raspberries, strawberries or red currants, cleaned sugar or honey

Preheat the oven to 300°F (150°C/Gas Mark 2). Make a caramel with the sugar and honey and pour a little into the bottom of each of 8 ramekins.

Beat together the eggs and honey. Scald the milk and stir it in to the eggs and honey mixture. Beat well to blend. Put the ramekins in a roasting pan (tin). Divide the custard between the ramekins and pour hot water into the roasting pan (tin) to come almost to the rims of the ramekins.

Bake the custards for 40–50 minutes, until just set and no longer wobbly when nudged. Leave them to cool in the turned-off oven, then chill.

Purée the fruit with sugar or honey to taste. Push through a fine strainer (sieve) to eliminate seeds or pips. Serve with the custards.

Mary Degen's Yeast Cake

This recipe for *Bienenstich* (meaning literally 'bee sting') is traditional throughout southern Germany, Switzerland and Alsace. Lovely for tea, split and spread with pastry cream, or on its own for breakfast.

Serves 6

2 cups (8oz/250g) flour
¼ tsp salt
¼ cup (2oz/50g) sugar
grated rind (zest) of ½ lemon
¼ cup (2oz/50g) soft butter
1 envelope (½oz/7g) instant-blending dry yeast or ½oz (15g)
fresh yeast
scant 1 cup (7fl oz/200ml) milk
1 egg, beaten

Topping
¼ cup (2oz/50g) butter
5 tbsp honey
75g/2½oz sliced (flaked) almonds

Mix together the flour, salt, sugar and lemon rind (zest). Work in the butter as if making pastry dough. If using dry yeast, add it now. If using fresh yeast dissolve it in the milk and add to the dry ingredients. Add the egg and beat well to a smooth, thick batter.

Encase the bowl in a plastic bag and leave the batter to rise at room temperature about 2 hours, until doubled in bulk.

Line the bottom of an 8-in (20-cm) spring-form cake pan (tin) with non-stick paper and butter the sides well.

Deflate the batter and pour it into the pan. Melt the butter and honey together, stir in the almonds, then cool a little.

Meanwhile, pre-heat the oven to 400°F (200°C/Gas Mark 6).

Spoon the mixture over the batter and bake for 25–30 minutes, or until golden brown and well risen. If the almonds are getting too brown, cover with a piece of foil.

Hazelnut Honey Cake

In this moist and delicious fatless sponge, the combination of nuts and honey gives a wonderful result. It is better still the day after baking. If you like, you can spread or sandwich it with a honey and cream cheese icing: 3½oz (100g) cream cheese beaten with 5 tbsp honey and a little lemon juice.

Serves 4–6

7½ tbsp runny honey
3 eggs, separated
½ cup (2oz/50g) flour
⅓ cup (2oz/50g) hazelnuts, finely ground
pinch salt

Preheat the oven to 350°F (180°C/Gas Mark 4). Line a 7-in (18-cm) spring-form cake pan (tin) with non-stick baking paper. Butter and flour the sides.

Beat together the honey and egg yolks until thoroughly mixed, light and fluffy. Sift the flour and fold it into the eggs and honey with the ground hazelnuts. Beat the egg whites with a pinch of salt until stiff but still creamy. Fold them into the cake mixture, then pour into the pan and bake for 30–35 minutes, or until golden brown, well risen and a needle inserted in the centre comes out clean.

Badger Crunch

Badgers, as is known, like honey almost as much as bears. In this recipe, also known as granola, a mixture of honey, oil and water is added to cereals, flour, nuts and seeds and baked to a crunch. It gives a breakfast cereal with considerably more character than muesli—just add yogurt or milk; or serve it on its own as a snack. For simplicity, the quantities are given in cups (any cup will do, as long it's the same one throughout.)

Makes about 6 cups

3 cups oatmeal (rolled oats)
$\frac{1}{2}$ cup whole-wheat (wholemeal) flour
$\frac{1}{2}$ cup rolled wheat flakes
$\frac{1}{2}$ cup sunflower or sesame seeds
$\frac{1}{2}$ cup milk powder
$\frac{1}{2}$ cup shredded coconut
$\frac{1}{2}$ cup bran
1 tsp salt
$\frac{1}{2}$ cup tasteless oil
$\frac{1}{2}$ cup runny honey
$\frac{1}{4}$ cup water
1 tsp vanilla extract (essence)
dried fruit of your choice, such as raisins, apricots and
banana chips (optional)

In a large roasting pan (tin) or baking tray with a lip, mix together the oats, flour, wheat flakes, sunflower or sesame seeds, milk powder, coconut, bran and salt. In a small pan, heat together the oil, honey, water and vanilla. Stir it into the dry ingredients, mixing well.

Preheat the oven to 325°F (170°C/Gas Mark 3).

Bake the crunch for 15 minutes, then take it out and stir it up well. Return to the oven for a further 15 minutes. Remove and leave to cool, then stir in dried fruit if wished. Keep in an airtight tin.

BIBLIOGRAPHY

Alphandéry, Ed. & Toulouse, C., *Le Miel, ses Usages et ses*
— *Propriétés*, E. Alphandéry Editeur, Avignon, 1912
Carper, Jean, *The Food Pharmacy*, Bantam, 1988
Casaulta, Gliecs, Krieg, Josef, Spiess, Walter, *Der*
Schweizerische Bienenvater, Verlag Sauerländer, 1985
Crane, Eva, *A Book of Honey*, Oxford University Press, 1980
— *The Archaeology of Beekeeping*, Duckworth, 1984
Diemer, Irmgard, *Bienen*, Franckh'sche Verlagshandlung,
1986
Edwardes, Tickner, *The Bee-Master of Warrilow*, Methuen,
1920
Herold, Edmund, *Heilwerte aus dem Bienenvolk*, Ehrenwirth
Verlag, 1970
Honey from Hive to Market, Bulletin No. 134, MAFF,
H.M.S.O., 1957
Das Kochbuch der Römer, Rezepte au Apicius, Artemis
Verlag, 1970
de Layens, Georges & Bonnier, Gaston, *Cours Complet*
d'Apiculture et Conduite d'un Rucher Isolé, Lib. Générale
de l'Enseignement
Majno, Guido, *The Healing Hand, Man and Wound in the*
Ancient World, Harvard University Press, 1975
Lerner, Franz, *Blüten, Nektar, Bienenfleiss*, Ehrenwirth
Verlag, 1984
McGee, Harold, *On Food and Cooking*, Allen & Unwin,
1984
Melzer, Werner, *Bienenhaltung*, Gräfe und Unzer, 1986
ed. Morse, Roger and Hooper, Ted, *The Illustrated*
Encyclopaedia of Beekeeping, Blandford Press, Poole,
Dorset, 1985
Moritz, Robin, *Der Hobby-Imker*, Falken Verlag, 1988
Rowsell, Henry and MacFarlane, Helen, *Henry's Bee Herbal*,
Thorsons, 1974
Sinclair, W., *Life of the Honey-bee*, Ladybird, 1969
Virgil, *The Georgics*, Trans. L. P. Wilkinson, Penguin, 1982

INDEX